1750

GREEN GROWS THE CITY

BEVERLEY NICHOLS

GREEN
GROWS THE
CITY

*The Story of a London
Garden*

ANTIQUE COLLECTORS' CLUB

ISBN 1 870673 23 9

First published in 1939
by Jonathan Cape Ltd., London and Toronto
Reprinted in 1997 by the Antique Collectors' Club Ltd.

British Library Cataloguing-in-Publication Data
A catalogue record for this book is available from the British Library

Printed in England
on Consort Royal Era Satin from Donside Mills, Aberdeen
by the Antique Collectors' Club Ltd., Woodbridge, Suffolk

Other books by

BEVERLEY NICHOLS

Fiction

SELF

PATCHWORK

PRELUDE

FOR ADULTS ONLY

CRAZY PAVEMENTS

EVENSONG

REVUE

General

TWENTY-FIVE

THE STAR-SPANGLED MANNER

ARE THEY THE SAME AT HOME?

WOMEN AND CHILDREN LAST

CRY HAVOC!

THE FOOL HATH SAID

NO PLACE LIKE HOME

NEWS OF ENGLAND

Chronicles of Allways

DOWN THE GARDEN PATH

A THATCHED ROOF

A VILLAGE IN A VALLEY

Omnibus

OXFORD-LONDON-HOLLYWOOD

Drama

FAILURES

MESMER

CONTENTS

To
My Friends Next Door

INTRODUCTION

ONCE I wrote another book about another garden. And friends who have peered over my shoulder while the story of *Green Grows the City* was unfolding itself have suggested that some of the figures who wandered down the path of that earlier garden have strayed — absent-mindedly, of course, without quite realizing what they were doing — on to the tiny lawn outside my present window. 'But Mrs. H. is none other than Mrs. M.!' they have exclaimed. 'And Héloise is our old friend Undine! You are a fraud. We thought that these were real people. And now, it seems, you were making them up, all the time.'

Well, perhaps I was. Maybe Mrs. H. *is* Mrs. M. Maybe Héloise, even if she did not flutter from exactly the same nest as Undine, is a bird of very similar plumage. If you come to this conclusion, I do not see why you should blame me for it, any more than that you should blame me for carrying down from my old garden the many seeds and plants and shrubs which are now flowering . . . not quite so freely, but no less sweetly . . . under the smoky skies of London.

I have been wondering to whom this book should be dedicated. To my real neighbours, I think, with whom I have always had the happiest relationships, on both sides of the fence.

CHAPTER I

WE MOVE IN

'I GIVE IT UP,' I said to Gaskin, throwing myself into a chair. 'If I look at any more houses I shall go mad. *You* must go and find one.'

Gaskin politely suggested that he had enough to do, running one house, and attending to the complex needs of its owner, without going in search of another.

'It can't be helped. I'll dine out. You can send my clothes to that man at the end of the street. And Mrs. Thing can come in and tidy up.'

Dismay was registered on Gaskin's face at the first two suggestions. It turned to disgust at the mention of Mrs. Thing. In icy tones he gave me to understand that if Mrs. Thing were so much as to set foot in his kitchen, he himself would be reluctantly compelled to fly out of the window.

'Well then, if you don't like Mrs. Thing, get someone else. There must be dozens. The main thing is that you've got to look for a house.'

He elevated his eyebrows. There was otherwise no sign of emotion.

I reached for the evening newspaper. (The meanness, the baseness of employers, when they wish to avoid an argument in which they know they will be

worsted!) 'And now,' — as though the subject were
dismissed, 'I should like a Bronx.'

'Large?' There was a world of meaning in the way he
said that word.

'Yes, please. Very large indeed.'

§ 11

I had a hunger for green. I was lonely for the sound of
trees by night. I longed for the feel of turf beneath my
feet, instead of the eternal pavement. Even if it were
only a narrow strip of sooty grass, it would be resilient
and alive, and would give me some of its own life.

I had never felt like this before. In the old days,
when I had been able to spend half my time in the
country, the city had seemed swift and colourful and
stimulating. If you have run through fields and walked
between hedges, from Friday till Tuesday, you have a
reserve of strength which carries you down the longest,
darkest streets. If your lungs have been filled with clean
air, tinged with all the exquisite scents of the land, the
scent of moss after rain, of beanfields in the evening
of the smoke of burning apple-wood, of the indescribable
fragrance that lingers, like an incantation, over a new-
mown lawn . . . if for whole days you have been tasting
these delights, then the breath of the city has no power
to stifle you, to sicken you with the poisons that it
perpetually distils.

But if you are hemmed in by bricks and mortar, week after week, as I was now, your powers of resistance are slowly sapped, till a sort of hysteria overcomes you. The city becomes a prison. The houses are the prison walls, the chimneys are the spikes, every citizen is a warder, and even the sky is barred with smoke.

To that pitch had I arrived. It was the same sort of neurosis that causes American citizens suddenly to flee from a comfortable apartment off Park Avenue and precipitate themselves into an uncomfortable attic over-looking Central Park. Anything for a little green. It is the spirit which makes men bankrupt themselves over a pent-house, expending more care and anxiety on a few vines and a tiny bed of bulbs than on the physical and mental welfare of their wives. Pent-house, pre-sumably, means a house for people who are pent. If it doesn't, it should.

At any rate, I was feeling so pent that if I stayed any longer in this little house in Westminster, something would explode. Westminster! How pleasant it had been to see that name on one's notepaper. It suggested vaguely that one had something to do with the House of Commons (though in fact, I was more closely situated to the Gas Light and Coke Company). It hinted at top hats moving through the spring shadows of the plane trees in Smith Square ... top hats that drifted down Lord North Street just before 1.30, and floated on to a little Sheraton table, while their owners went upstairs to lunch with Lady Colefax. A lovely name, Westminster.

It suggested Winston Churchill, archbishops, bells at night, schoolboys scrambling for pancakes, the grey hurrying waters of the Thames. It suggested a famous Duke, and quite a number of Duchesses. A hallowed name, you will agree.

But a nasty, damp, dirty, foggy hole of a place, if you ask me. If you climb up on the roofs of some of those quaint Georgian houses . . . roofs that look as though they had been designed by Walt Disney for the especial delectation of dwarfs, witches and poltergeists, you will see some of the gloomiest back yards in England. Over these backyards (and over the Georgian houses too), there creep the grey and poisonous vapours of the Thames. In fact, I had come to the conclusion that every fog in London started at my front door. A little yellow cloud, no bigger than a man's hand, hovering just over my letter-box, and then spreading swiftly down the street, flowing into the great square, drifting up to the summits of the plane trees, and then, away over London, to stop the traffic, tickle a million throats, and depress a million souls.

No. *J'en avais assez.*

§ I I I

A night passes, and a day. And I am sitting in the same chair, regarding Gaskin with an expression of incredulity, almost of dismay. For these are the words that he has just uttered:

'I think I have found what you want, sir.'

'You think . . .'

Words failed me. It was impossible. He had not left the house till eleven (in his determination to give no cause for the arrival of Mrs. Thing). Allowing him half an hour to get up to Heathstead, which was the neighbourhood I desired, half an hour to return, half an hour at the agents, and half an hour for lunch, he would have had exactly three hours in which to conduct his search. And I had already been at it for three months.

It was more than impossible. It was positively irritating.

'I don't see how you could have done that already,' I observed.

For reply he handed me a printed agent's form, giving particulars of Number 5, Highways Close, Heathstead.

'Have you seen it?'

'Oh, yes. It's a very nice little house.'

'Modern?'

'Yes. But very pretty.'

I sniffed, and studied the form. 'It's not freehold. I wanted a freehold.'

'It's a 999 years lease. I thought that might perhaps be sufficient.'

'It doesn't say anything about a garage.'

'There's a nice little garage.'

'How high up is the house?'

'Four hundred and sixteen feet above sea level.'

It was evidently impossible to defeat Gaskin. I made a last effort.

'There's no garden, of course?'

'There's a nice little garden.'

I gave it up. 'All right, I suppose there's no harm in seeing it.' And added, somewhat ungraciously, 'Thank you very much'.

§ I V

The suburb of Heathstead lies high above London, higher, so the inhabitants tell us, than the top of St. Paul's Cathedral, which rises to the dizzy eminence of three hundred and sixty-five feet. Be that as it may, the air is so sweet and clean that you cannot believe you are near a city at all. Often, when London is groping in a fog, Heathstead is sparkling in the sunshine. Fogs do reach us sometimes, but usually by the time they get to the top of the hill, they have shed much of their viciousness, and appear only as an amiable mist, which looks quite pretty, shrouding the trees and drifting over the roof of the old church.

So the first thing you must always say, when you come to lunch with an inhabitant of Heathstead, is . . . 'Oh, the *air*!' You must say this at once, loudly, and with great conviction. Otherwise, you will be thought impolite, if not a little queer in the head.

And the next thing you must say is . . . 'But I'd no idea it was so close to London.' No. Forgive me. That is what you must *not* say. We *are* London. I cannot think how I slipped into such an elementary error. What you must say is . . . 'I'd no idea it was so close to A. or B.', naming the particular district of the city you live in. After which you must add, if you wish to create a really good impression . . . 'Why, it only took me ten minutes from Piccadilly.' The fact that you know, and your host knows, that it took you a good twenty-five, only makes your remark the more gracious.

Needless to say, on this first afternoon, I was not in a very gracious mood. I was still smarting under a sense of inferiority, because Gaskin had found a house in three hours, while I had not found one in three months. And though I was in a state of anxiety bordering on desperation (for the lease at Westminster had only another six weeks to run) I could not suppress a sneaking hope that perhaps this house might be just as bad as all the others. 'The drains,' I decided. 'That must be the snag. And anyway, one can always *say* the drains are wrong. By the time it's been proved that they're not, the first flush of Gaskin's triumph will have worn off.'

It took us less than half an hour, at the busiest time of the day, from Westminster. Or if you prefer it, twenty minutes from Hyde Park Corner, or ten minutes from Baker Street. So I couldn't complain about that. Nor about the strangely 'country' feeling that assailed you as soon as you swept up the hill. Nor about the unbroken quietness of the road into which we suddenly turned at the top.

'It's there,' said Gaskin, pointing to the bottom of the road.

'Where?' All I saw was some trees.

'Just in the hollow, round the corner.'

There was something very pleasant about that phrase, 'just in the hollow round the corner'. It may not have had the evocative magic of 'over the hills and far away', which is, of course, the most beautiful line in English poetry. But it had a nice, comforting sound.

And sure enough, there it was, or rather, there they were. 'Just in the hollow round the corner.' Five little houses, cunningly tucked away from the rest of the road. Not joined together. Oh dear, no, nothing so common as that. At least, not really joined together — only in a sort of Siamese-twin way. By which I mean that the houses *looked* quite detached, and it was only when you studied them very carefully that you saw a minor architectural feature, like a sort of arch, which linked each one to its neighbour.

'Well, it's certainly quiet enough,' I agreed.

It was indeed. Although the great avenue at the top of the hill, with its incessant roar of traffic hurtling to the North, was a bare hundred yards away, the steep gradient of Highways Road had the effect of dulling the roar into a faint and not unpleasing murmur. The moment that you stepped round the corner into the Close itself, even this murmur was lost. Instead, you suddenly became aware of all sorts of country sounds that you thought you had forgotten for ever; the sound of thrushes scurrying through the undergrowth, of the creak of branches rubbing together in the wind, of the soft patter of rain-drops on a pile of dying leaves.

As we stood there, a distant clock struck five. I looked up and saw about a quarter of a mile away the tall spire of Heathstead church rising from a nest of trees. For a moment I wondered if I should express to Gaskin a mythical anxiety about those chimes, if I should suggest that they would undoubtedly keep us awake at night. I had not the heart to do so. They rang so sweetly on this autumn evening; they reminded me of another church I had known, long ago. It was astonishing that one heard them so clearly.

'It's even quieter at Number Five,' said Gaskin.

So it proved to be. The drive of the Close made a sharp curve. And there at the end was Number 5. A simple little house; one might almost say a demure little house, with a roof of red tiles and apple-green shutters round the windows.

'I thought you said there was a garden?'

'It's on the other side.'

'Let's go in and see.'

We went in. But we did not look at the garden just yet. Indeed, I purposely avoided doing so, for the house itself was such fun. There was one long airy room, full of light, which would be perfect for music. A small dining-room adjoined it. There was a study that looked out on to the shrubbery in front. There were three bedrooms and two bathrooms, and lots of cupboards. And the

23

whole thing was gay and sensible and the sort of place that people should live in.

'I think it's grand,' I said to Gaskin. 'And now let's look at the garden.'

It was at this point that Gaskin showed his quality by withdrawing, on the pretext that he wished to acquaint himself with certain mysteries of the kitchen. For he somehow sensed, with a tact that would have done credit to a great many of his so-called 'superiors', that this was a rather difficult moment for me. With my memories of another garden, I think we *can* say it was difficult, without being accused of sentimentality.

§ v

'Good God!'

I stared out of the window. The light was fading fast, it had begun to rain hard, and the wind was rising, scattering handfuls of leaves from an immense weeping willow in the garden next door. It would have been a melancholy prospect, at the best of times, to watch from an empty unheated house. But it was not with the fall of the leaves, nor with the fall of the rain, nor with the fall of the day nor the year, that my heart fell also at that moment. It was because this 'garden' was the ugliest, most desolate strip of ground that can ever have been trodden by human feet, outside the no man's land of the Great War.

To begin with, it was a stark, uncompromising triangle, of which the house formed the base. You looked out on to two wooden fences (of the mass-produced, creosoted variety), which started at each side of the house, and ran towards each other for about twenty yards, colliding in a sharp and angry apex at the top.

You will be hearing so much about this triangle, in the later pages of the book, that I have put in a photograph of it, in order that you may see that I am not exaggerating. It is called, 'As it was in the Beginning', and should face page 24 , unless the binders get tangled up in the machinery. Even this photograph, revolting as it is, does not convey the full horror of the picture as it met my eyes on that gloomy October afternoon. For one thing, brick walls have replaced the wooden fences (though you will observe that the left-hand wall is not yet completed). For another, there is a little terrace, which does at least give you something to step on to, instead of the sea of mud which was there originally. Finally, in the photograph you are spared the sight of three gaunt blackened poplar stumps which used to stand in the apex, emphasizing the triangularity of the whole design.

As I stood at the window it was upon those poplar stumps that my attention fixed itself. If I had known that they were to be the centre of a fierce drama before many weeks had passed, I might have regarded them even more intently. How monstrous they were! Six foot apiece, beheaded, with a few diseased shoots sticking out of the tops, straight up in the air. They looked like the skeletons of umbrellas blown inside out by the wind. And arranged in a triangle — as if the garden were not triangular enough already.

Garden! If one were given to producing the noise which is known in fiction as a 'hollow laugh', this would have been an occasion for giving the hollowest laugh that has ever echoed over the city of London. Garden! I stepped outside. Deep into the mud. Right over the ankles. Some planks had been left by the builders and I made a precarious progress on them towards the apex.

I turned round. Well, at any rate we weren't as 'overlooked' as I had feared. And from this point you forgot about the triangle. But the idea that this fantastically-shaped patch of nothing at all could ever be made into anything but a cat-run . . . well, it was too silly.

That was what it would have to be — a cat-run. Apart from this, it would be ignored. Thus resolved, I returned to the house.

'We'll take it,' I said to Gaskin, though with less enthusiasm than I might have shown five minutes before.

'You saw the garden, sir?'

'Yes. I saw it. It'll do nicely for the cats.'

We went outside, locked the door, and after a final look, began to walk back up the drive.

As we passed Number 1, I paused. It seemed, in some way, a little larger than the other houses. I wondered why. Then I saw that it had an extra chimney. What could be the reason for *that*? This was a mystery which would one day demand explanation.

But not yet. For it was not with the chimney of Number 1 that I was preoccupied, but with a gay, sunken garden outside its front door, separated from the drive by a wall about two feet high. Really, whoever lived there had taste. The garden was paved in a charming design, with numerous rock plants climbing in and out of the crevices. In the centre was an oblong pool in which a fountain was playing. In the water I could see an occasional gleam which implied the presence of goldfish.

I turned to Gaskin. 'I'm sure the fish can't like it in that pool.' A faint suspicion came to me. (Or perhaps they're made of celluloid?)

But no. The goldfish were moving. And it was too much to hope that they were mechanically propelled.

'I call it cruelty to animals.'

I was about to peer closer, when Gaskin's expression of dignified disapproval deterred me.

'What is it?'

He made no reply, but his eyes wandered, for a fraction of a second, to Number 1's upstairs windows. I followed his glance. Even as I looked, I saw a faint movement of a curtain, and the shadow of a woman with a very large nose. Discreetly, I turned away.

'Mrs. Heckmondwyke,' proclaimed Gaskin, in tones of cold contempt.

'Mrs. What?'

'Heckmondwyke,' he repeated. 'Very nosey.'

'Physically or mentally?'

'When I came with the keys yesterday, she stopped me in the drive, and asked me if she could come in for a minute. Said she'd always wanted to see what her garden looked like from over the wall.'

'And did you let her?'

'I did *not*.'

'Oh, Gaskin, do you think that was right?'

'Yes, sir, I *do*.'

'But what did you say? How could you stop her?'

'I told her that you had given strict orders that nobody else was to see over the house as long as you were considering it.'

'Oh, dear,' was all I could think of. It was very depressing. 'I hope we haven't made an enemy.'

Gaskin did not comment on this statement. His lips set in a firm line. 'I know the type,' he said.

'Yes, but she *is* a neighbour. And we have to live only four houses away from her.'

'Yes,' said Gaskin, 'she is. And we do.' Then, looking at me darkly, he proclaimed, 'I think, sir, that it will be best for you to keep yourself to yourself.'

Upon which, we drove back to Westminster.

CHAPTER II

HIGH WIND IN SUBURBIA

I MOVED into Highways Close at about the same time as Mussolini began to move into Abyssinia, which is not as irrelevant as it sounds, because one of the great things about moving into a new house is that it makes you forget the European situation. No other recipe is so effective. None of the other great motive forces of mankind, not love, nor jealousy, nor avarice, nor fear . . . none of these make you forget the European situation. They deepen your depression. Moving house is the only certain cure.

During the month which elapsed before moving day, the words which echoed most frequently in my ears were, 'I-do-not-wish-to-deter-you-sir, *but.*' These words, incredible as it may sound, came from Mr. Peregrine the decorator. Whenever I wanted to do anything absurd, such as knocking down the wall between the dining-room and the sitting-room, and building a bar out into the 'garden', Mr. Peregrine did-not-wish-to-deter-me, *but.*

'How do you make your living, Mr. Peregrine, if you are always deterring people?'

'I do not *wish* . . .' began Mr. Peregrine.

'I know, but you *do.* You've already deterred me from wasting at least a hundred pounds.'

29

Mr. Peregrine, who looks like an Ambassador to the Court of St. James's, merely shrugged his shoulders.

'You should egg people on, Mr. Peregrine. I would, if I were in your job.'

Mr. Peregrine affected not to believe this statement.

But it is true. I would egg people on like mad.

Anyway, in spite of the deterrent influence of Mr. Peregrine, I managed to spend quite a lot of money. You see, it was the first really modern house that I had ever owned, and I wanted to take advantage of this modernity. So the first thing I did was to buy a Frigidaire, which is still regarded by a large proportion of the British people as rather daring, even shocking. Like bloomers. This machine fills me with fascination, not unmingled with fear, to this day. Those cubes! Mysteriously forming in the depths of the night! That frost . . . out of the nowhere into here! I once wrote a story about a ghost in a Frigidaire, but it was so terrifying that it had to be set aside.

Then I bought a water-softener. A very civilizing influence it proved to be. And an electric fan, which had to be given away because the cats dabbed at it. And a coffee pot that whistled like a mad creature when its hour had come. There was no end to the things I bought.

But that was not the way in which most of the money was spent. No. Most of the money was spent in trying to make the house look as if nothing had been spent on it at all. You know the idea. Stark, naked simplicity. Sack-cloth curtains. Concealed lighting. One or two

huge arm-chairs. A piano in unpolished walnut. Otherwise, nothing. If, by any chance, you suffer from the
delusion that this sort of thing is cheap, please believe
me when I tell you that it is not. Nothing in decoration
costs as much as making a thing look like Nothing . . . if
it is the right sort of Nothing (the same applies to women's
clothes). It is cheaper to buy museum pieces, to cover
the floor with an Aubusson carpet, and to sprinkle the
walls with early Corots.

However, at last it was finished. The last piece of
Nothing was in place. The beds were aired. The only
thing to do was to move in. Which, to cut a long story
short, we did.

Now this, though you may not believe it, is a book
about a garden. So you shall be spared the story of a
number of adventures which might have been relevant
if it had been a book about a house.

During the following week Mr. Peregrine called to
investigate a leaking drain-pipe. In order to investigate
it properly, he had to step through the french windows of
the sitting-room, out into the triangle. I joined him,
having a keen interest in a drain-pipe which was to be
mine for 999 years.

The drain-pipe having yielded its secret, Mr. Peregrine
turned, and surveyed the triangle. Then he turned
again, and surveyed me. In the tone of one who addresses
a master, he said:

'I expect we shall be seeing great things *here*, sir.'

I did not get what he meant.

'We all know,' he said, 'how keen you are on gardening.'

This was very embarrassing. I tried to change the subject, without success.

'Have you any particular plans in mind, sir?'

'No. I'm afraid I haven't.'

'It's an awkward shape.'

'Yes. Very awkward.' I racked my brains for some idea. 'I suppose we could turf it,' I said, for the sake of saying something. 'And then . . .'

Mr. Peregrine waited, as though great words of wisdom were about to be uttered. But I could think of no words at all. The whole subject seemed unprofitable, and painful.

'And then,' I added, turning back into the house, 'you'd better cut down those three poplar stumps. They're an eyesore. And they're rather dangerous. We don't want them blowing down and breaking the fence.'

That, one would have thought, was an end of the matter. It proved to be only the beginning. In fact, you might almost describe it as the start of our whole story.

For the episode of the poplar stumps led me, for the first time, to realize that I was no longer living in the heart of the country, no longer master of all I surveyed. I was surrounded by quantities of small sovereign states, all intensely nationalist, and populated by mysterious and possibly hostile tribes who, in the history of Suburbia, are described by the generic term of 'Neighbours'.

§ I I

For a moment we must be topographical. It is a bore, but it is necessary.

Supposing you had entered my house, during that early period, and walked through the hall into the drawing-room, what would you have seen?

Obviously, the triangle, to begin with. You could not help seeing the triangle. It almost bit you.

Beyond the triangle, you would have seen nothing but trees (some of them very beautiful), with an occasional roof or gable peering through them, not too obtrusively. And then again, beyond the trees, far below, you would have seen ... London. A tumbled mass of roofs and spires and pinnacles, grey or glistening, according to the mood of the weather.

That was what you would have seen if you had kept your eyes front.

Now turn your head to the right. With pleasure you note that the only thing you see at first is a long, smooth lawn. It is big enough for a full-size tennis court, though I hope that nobody ever attempts to put one there. If you are lucky, you might see the Lady-Next-Door ... a graceful, elderly figure, who sometimes flits like a shadow across the lawn, picks a few flowers, and then flits back again. The Lady-Next-Door will play as little part in these pages as she has played in my life, and the role of the House-Next-Door (which is how the house on the right will be described) will be equally shadowy.

33

In fact, it is only because we are being topographical that I mention it at all.

And yet, in passing, is it not a strange thing, an almost uncanny thing, that so many millions of people live next door to each other, in the great cities, and remain utterly mysterious and unknown? The same rain falls on us, the same sun salutes us, we are shaken by the same fears and animated by the same hopes. Yet we remain apart, year after year. All we tell each other of ourselves is told by the drawing down of our blinds and the switching on, or off, of our lights. 'The Lady-Next-Door has come in . . . is going to bed . . . is getting up.' Of these things we may be reasonably certain. But what she thinks when she comes in, whether she is happy or sad when, for a moment, we see her face at the window, what life means to her, we shall never know. Yes, it is a strange thing, this city life, and it seems even stranger to those who have lived in a village, where we know more of the private life of the poorest family in the most remote cottage than we shall ever know of our neighbours in the city.

Well — we have looked to the right and we have looked to the front. Now let us look to the left. We shall see four little houses very much like our own, though some have sunblinds and others haven't, some have vines and creepers, others are bare. The houses are cleverly grouped, and so arranged that they do not seem to be overlooking each other. They all appear to be detached and they all have little gardens. Mine and Number 4 are the only houses which are cursed with a triangle.

My own house is Number 5. But perhaps it would be simpler if we put it like this:

We have already dealt with the House-Next-Door. Number 5, as you will note, is me. Number 4 we can pass by, except to observe that Mr. and Mrs. Howard are the owners of a magnificent weeping willow, which towers far above all our gardens, and affords a constant delight to most of us. It is not an unmitigated delight to the Howards, because its roots are old and greedy, and suck the nourishment out of their borders like any vampire. However, the Howards have no intention of cutting it down, for they are unselfish people. In fact, they are such ideal neighbours that there is little I can think of to say about them. 'Happy is the people that has no history.'

For the moment we can also pass by Numbers 3 and 2. But we cannot ignore Number 1. Not only because it is just a little grander than any of the other houses, with an extra chimney, a wider terrace, and a small 'water' garden in the front as well as at the back. Nor only because upon this 'water' garden Mrs. Heckmondwyke lavishes endless care and a quite indecent amount of money (and cheats, into the bargain, as we afterwards discovered. For in the season of water-lilies she goes to Woolworth's, buys artificial flowers which are intended to float in bowls on dining-tables, and cunningly arranges them among the broad, flat leaves. The result, I regret to say, is disgustingly realistic). Not for these reasons is it impossible to ignore Number 1, but for the simple reason that Number 1 apparently finds it impossible to ignore us.

Every time we walk past the front door, regarding that
blaze of spurious blossom with as much indifference as
is possible, even yawning in its face to show our contempt for it, there is a slight but perceptible movement
of the curtains upstairs. Mrs. Heckmondwyke is looking
out. And if by any chance, Mrs. H. is not at home,
there is the same slight but perceptible movement in the
curtains downstairs. Her Ada — the name by which
Mrs. H.'s cook is generally known — has taken up the
good work, and is keeping watch until such time as the
Commander-in-Chief returns. If there were a Mr. H.,
perhaps he too would take his turn as sentry. But there
is no Mr. H. Or rather, no Colonel H. For Mrs.
Heckmondwyke is the widow of an officer who died while
serving with His Majesty's forces in India. Incidentally,
she never forgets what is due to the importance of his
position.

But it is not only upon our persons that Mrs. H.
lavishes these flattering attentions. She is even more
enthralled by our gardens. Not a thing can be put in,
or pulled up, or pruned, or sprayed, without her knowing
about it. Not because she can overlook us; our gardens
are so arranged that we can all have our little bit of
privacy. She just seems to find out. If she were not so
very British in appearance, I would swear that she had
Red Indian blood in her veins, and spent her evenings
crouching behind laurels in peculiar positions, with one
ear to the ground.

Needless to say, none of these things were known to me

at the period of which I write. Neighbours do not call on one another, at any rate in England, not even when they are living in a Close. In America, I suppose, they would be in and out of each other's houses all day. But in England, for the first six months, when we meet our next-door neighbour, we take one glance at him and then look away in great embarrassment, as though he had forgotten to do up some essential portion of his clothing. During the next six months, one or two smirks may be permitted, accompanied by a movement of the lips. We do not actually say 'Good morning' or 'How are you?' That would be 'forward'. We make a faint noise which, if recorded on a gramophone, would sound like a sigh of pain. Which in a sense it is . . . pain at the thought of the ordeal that awaits us in the years to come, the ordeal of actually introducing ourselves!

It takes a great catastrophe, like a war or a general strike, or some untoward manifestation of Nature, to break the social ice of the English suburbs.

And so it was in this case. It was a high wind that did it. Or if it was not the wind itself, the tempest within was so intimately connected with the tempest without, that it amounts to the same thing.

§III

I love wind. Out here, high up above the city, where the air is so clean and buoyant, I love it most of all. On the day of which I am writing the air was full of flying leaves. The willow at Number 4 was scattering a largesse of silver, the planes in the House-Next-Door were clinging desperately to the last shreds of their tattered clothing, the poplars, scattered all over the hill, were in a state of the greatest agitation, bending this way and that, as if they would have flown from this terror if they had not been tied by the roots. Almost the only tree that seemed to be holding its own was the great copper beech, in a distant garden whose owner I have never discovered. Not a leaf did it shed. It gave the impression of vast reserves, as though nothing would ever make it desert the bronze standard.

I pressed my nose to the window, looking out. In this uproar it was possible to forget the triangle. It seemed to be swallowed up in mightier things, overshadowed by the troops of scudding clouds, by the whirling arms of great branches. Even the sense that the little house was defending itself made you forget the triangle. There was the sound of windows banging of their own accord, of a slate being blown loose, of a pane of glass smashed in the distance by the fragment of a branch.

And there was the sound of the front door bell.

'Out!' I croaked to Gaskin, opening the door the fraction of an inch and then closing it again.

But he was back immediately. 'Mrs. Heckmondwyke,' he whispered.

'Who is Mrs. Heckmondwyke?'

Signs. Movements of the head. She was in the hall. She could hear.

'What does she want?'

'She says it's very important. Very urgent indeed.'

Grindings of teeth. Secret resolutions for subterranean exits. 'Oh, very well.'

She entered the room breathlessly. I didn't wonder. The wind was enough to knock any woman off her feet.

We greeted each other. Yes. It was the same woman whose shadow I had seen behind the curtain, on the day we first inspected the house. She was very tall, about fifty, with grey hair, a thin mouth, and a nose which her admirers might call 'patrician', though it reminded me of the Duke of Wellington. She had a flat chest, large feet, and a husky voice. She seemed to be a lady. Yes. That is what she seemed to be.

'I must apologize,' she said, or rather, gulped. 'Bursting in like this.' And before I had time to murmur any reply, she hurried to the window and looked out. 'Ah!' she cried, 'they're still there!'

I followed the direction of her eyes. I could see nobody in the triangle. 'Who?' I asked.

'My trees!'

'Your trees!' I was puzzled. As far as I could see from this distance, over three intervening gardens, nothing had happened, or seemed likely to happen, to Mrs. Heckmondwyke's trees. True, the wind was increasing at every moment, and was making them sway about in great agitation. But they were stoutly rooted, and could stand up to a lot more punishment.

'I don't think you need worry,' I said. 'They look all right to me.'

'They do?' she cried eagerly. 'They really do?'

Had she by any chance taken perhaps a little too much to drink? Her behaviour was so very unexpected. But not nearly as unexpected as her next remark.

'Then you've changed your mind? You really have?'

I blinked. One of us, certainly, was mad. 'Changed my mind? About what?'

'About my trees!' Her voice rose almost to a wail. 'They told me you were going to cut them down.'

'But Mrs. Heckmondwyke . . . by the way, won't you please sit down? . . . how could I possibly cut down your trees? I've got nothing whatever to do with them.'

She smiled faintly. (But she did sit down.) 'Foolish of me,' she said. 'Naturally, you wouldn't understand. I mean *your* trees.'

Curiouser and curiouser. 'But I haven't any trees. Only those three old poplar stumps.'

'Those beautiful poplars,' she sighed, almost to herself. 'Part of my life.'

'I don't think we can be talking about the same trees,' I said.

'Oh, yes!' She nodded, several times. 'Oh, yes, we are. Though perhaps not in the same spirit.'

This really seemed to me intolerable. First of all, to be told that my three poplar stumps were 'her' trees. Secondly, to be told that they were beautiful, when they were hideous, misshapen and diseased. Thirdly, to be told, even indirectly, that I was incapable of appreciating them. I was about to indicate as much, when she interrupted. Holding up her hand, she said:

'Year after year, I've looked out of my window and seen those poplars, waving in the wind.'

'But Mrs. Heckmondwyke, how could they wave in the wind? They each consist of a black stump, about six feet high . . .'

'In the wind,' she repeated, in a sort of trance.

'On top of which,' I continued, with growing spirit, 'there are at the most six shoots, which are extremely unsightly.'

'I've painted those trees,' she interrupted. Not quite so dreamily.

'I think you might have chosen a more pleasing subject.'

Her eyes narrowed. 'In water colours,' she observed. Not at all dreamy, now.

'I'm sure the pictures are charming,' I snapped. 'But if so, they must be highly impressionistic.'

We glared at each other in silence. This was terrible. I had no doubt that I was being rude, but the provocation was extreme.

Mrs. H. made as though she were going to speak, and then thought better of it. She forced a smile, inclined her head, and walked to the door.

'Please,' she said, 'don't trouble to show me out.'

Naturally I did not avail myself of this suggestion. I opened the door for her. I bowed. She bowed. The wind was so strong that it almost bumped our heads together. But I was grateful to it. For it blew Mrs. H. almost bodily down the steps and up the drive. And for the moment, out of my life.

CHAPTER III

FALSE START

IN spite of this passage at arms, the trees came down the next day. 'Came down', indeed, is hardly the right way to put it. They were so rotten that they only needed a slight tug to lift them out of the ground. It was pleasing to note that the roots were yellow, mildewed, and writhing with wire-worms. In order that Mrs. Heckmondwyke might be acquainted with this fact, I caused the trees to be laid at the edge of the drive, with the roots pointing in her direction. There they remained until nightfall.

A week later, I decided to follow the example of the other residents of the Close, and to lay down a little terrace. This was done without any idea of making a 'garden', and certainly without any great enthusiasm. The only reason for the terrace was to have a place where one could prowl up and down in fine weather.

However, one thing leads to another, and having achieved the terrace, it seemed foolish not to turf the rest of the garden. It was not much fun prowling up and down by the side of a lot of mud and rubble.

This turfing proved to be a much more expensive job than I had anticipated. However horrible the triangle might be, there was no point in putting good turf on to soil that was not fit to receive it. So one day I borrowed a fork and began to dig. Half an hour's digging was enough to prove that the soil was the sort of stuff that the lowest stinging nettle would refuse to grow on. It needed weeks of treatment. It got it.

That soil was turned over, every inch of it, to a depth of two feet. From every square foot came a pile of rubbish — bricks, tin cans, broken china and the like. By the time we were through, we had disposed of a lorry-load of miscellaneous junk, including such unlikely objects as the top of a statuette of Napoleon.

When the soil had had the benefit of several heavy frosts, I sent for Mr. Peregrine, and gave him instructions for a simple but effective method of drainage. (As this was a matter of gardening, a subject of which I was supposed to have some knowledge, he showed no desire to deter me, which was a great relief.)

Finally, the soil being reasonably friable, I dug in a sack of lime and three whole sacks of bone-meal (of which I am a confirmed and hopeless addict). After which, there was nothing to do but to send for the turf, and lay it.

And then — to forget the whole thing once more.

§ 11

That, at least, was the intention. But it was not so easy to forget. Not because the laying of the turf had awakened

45

any ambitions to go a little further, to make a bed or two, or even to plant a few shrubs. For precisely the opposite reason. The laying of the turf had only served to emphasize the obvious triangularity of the land. In the days when it had been nothing but a mud-heap, it had been comparatively bearable. But now, the bright green turf made it seem so sharp and pointed that it began to get on my nerves.

I tried to ignore it, but it refused to be ignored. Even when I was not looking at it, I knew that it was looking at me. If you think that is a sign of undue sensitivity, you are wrong. For if the desk at which you work looks straight on to two wooden fences, converging into an apex, those fences seem gradually to advance upon you, to come closer, as though they had taken a mysterious shuffle forward during the night. At first I thought that this might actually have happened, and that somebody might be rooting up the fence and pushing it a few inches further forward in order to increase his own property. I decided that it must be an optical delusion.

However, this did not make it any more bearable. Now and then I would look out of the window — not because there was anything to see, but simply in order to rest my eyes — and each time that I did so I felt the impending advent of a squint. The right wall seemed to take hold of one eye and the left wall of the other, compelling them to cross each other and to focus on that horrible little apex at the end.

One dreary afternoon in February, the thing became

unbearable. *Something* would have to be done about this
garden, even if it were only to build a high brick wall
right round it. Better to look out on a brick wall than
on two wooden fences that made you squint. So I
threw down my pen, put on an overcoat, and went
outside.

As usual, my mind became a blank. There just wasn't
anything to do about it.

'Dreaming?'

It was a high feminine voice just behind me. One of
those voices which to the owner suggests the flute, but to
the listener, the piccolo.

I turned round. It was Héloise. To be precise,
Héloise Sumner-James. This is not her real name, but it
gives much the same effect. She was tall, willowy, and
dark. And if you like girls who look as if they spent much
of their leisure in their bedrooms, wearing Spanish
shawls and very little else, posing in front of triple mirrors,
biting cabbage carnations between their pearly teeth,
under the illusion that they look like Spanish señoritas . . .
if you happen to like this type, then I suppose you would
call Héloise beautiful.

Héloise is now far, far away. (I don't mean that she is
dead. It is a mere matter of mileage.) But were she
standing behind me at this moment, I should continue to
write about her, in the certain knowledge that she is too
conceited to recognize herself. Even if she did, she would
smile loftily, and say that she was glad that she had given
me a type (pronounced teep).

And she really *would* be glad. Héloïse's unconquerable optimism was the most maddening thing about her. She was the gladdest girl you ever met. Glad about Life, in all its aspects. And at this moment, very very Glad about me.

'Dreaming?' she repeated, tripping gladly forwards into the mud.

I wondered how she had got in. Gaskin must have left the front door open for the cats. Memo: Have special cat-door made in kitchen within forty-eight hours.

'No,' I snapped ungraciously. (If one had a cat-door in the kitchen, one would have to put Cavalier's dinner on the top of the gas-stove. Otherwise, strange cats would arrive. Which would be enchanting for me, but not for Cavalier.)

'But you *are*,' she cried. 'I'll fly!' She turned. Her foot, which was rather elegant, squelched in the mud. She drew it out. Gladly.

'Please don't,' I muttered. (Manners getting worse every day, I thought. Perhaps one could have the cat door higher up, so that only Cavalier could reach it? But no. That would be unkind.)

'No,' I repeated. 'Please don't go. Perhaps you might give me some ideas.'

She opened her eyes very wide. Oh, how Glad she was! Her lips parted. 'About . . . ?' she breathed.

'About triangles.'

Her eyelids fluttered. Something, she knew, was coming. So it was incumbent upon her only to balance

48

in the mud, flutter, and hope that it would come before she sank any deeper.

I put her out of her agony. I told her the problem. How to turn a triangle into a square, or a circle, or a rhomboid, or anything but what it was.

'It *is* difficult,' she mused, looking at the horrid prospect before her. 'But then' — (turning, Glad again) — 'that only makes it all the more fun, don't you think?'

'No, I don't, really.'

'Oh, but you *do*. You, of all people, must see that.'

'The fact remains that I don't.'

'Ah . . . but you *will*! You'll make something beautiful of it!' she exclaimed.

'But how, Héloise?'

'Don't ask *me*!' she tinkled. 'I'm not a creator. I'm just *me*.'

There seemed to be no point in denying these statements, which were both true. So I remained silent.

She rattled her bangles, clasped her hands, and gazed at the mud-patch. 'It will come,' she sighed.

'What?'

'It! The Great It. One day you will be walking over this little wilderness, and you'll see It. And then! How *glad* you'll be that it was all so difficult!'

Here she was, thrusting her gladness on to me. It was too much. I proposed that we should go in and have some tea.

§III

In spite of Héloise, I was determined to do something about the garden before it was dark, even if I did something quite wrong. We could not go on like this. So after she had departed, I went round to Number 4 to ask Mrs. Howard if I might borrow her gardener for a little while.

'Of course,' she said readily. 'He's just finished. Joseph!'

Joseph appeared. A pleasant young man. Who became even pleasanter when he discovered that one really did know a few things about gardening. Within a couple of minutes we were standing in the middle of the triangle, making plans for the summer.

'There's very little to be done with a patch of this shape,' I said. I hoped that perhaps Joseph might make some suggestion. But all he did was to scratch his head, and agree that, as far as he could see, there was nothing anybody could do except tidy it up.

'So all I want you to do is to stick in a few small trees just to soften it down.'

Actually we did a little more than that. I arranged for three silver birches in the centre, one or two standard flowering mays on the left side, a pink almond on the right, and two weeping crabs in front of the house. It seemed rather silly to have no flowers at all, so I told him to make a border on the right, and fill it with Siberian wallflowers.

'Nothing else, sir? That'd make a nice place for any herbaceous stuff.'

It was rather an effort not to speak sharply to Joseph when he said that, not to tell him that I'd once had herbaceous borders which were the best in the county, and that the idea of making a parody of a herbaceous border in this squalid strip of London earth was repulsive. However, Joseph couldn't be expected to know all that. So I checked myself, and said no, we'd just have the wallflowers. If he felt like it he might naturalize a few bulbs in the grass. That was all.

'And what about the point at the end, sir? That's the sharpest bit of all.'

I'd forgotten the apex. To tell the truth the whole discussion was a little boring. It seemed so futile. All the same, we went down to look at it.

It was this shape:

It was a horrible little corner. Knowing what it is to-day, remembering the many hours of keen delight spent in that same tiny area, it seems almost impossible to believe that the scene I am describing ever took place at all. And yet it did. I stared about me. It was un-utterably depressing. It wasn't even a proper triangle.

'I feel like cutting the whole thing off and making a present of it to the lady at Number 1,' I said.

'Oh, I wouldn't do *that*, sir,' exclaimed Joseph in a shocked voice. 'I wouldn't give anything to the lady at Number 1.'

Remembering the episode of the trees, I was inclined to agree with Joseph.

'But what *can* we do with it?'

'It would make a nice place for rhododendrons,' said Joseph.

§ I V

Looking back on it to-day, I believe that it was Joseph's casual remark about the rhododendrons which was really the beginning of it all. For that remark evoked a host of memories, so deep and so poignant that they revived something in me which I thought had died for ever. They made me realize that I should never be happy unless some part of me were in the earth . . . that I must have roots . . . and that if one foot at least was not in the soil, the other most assuredly would be in the grave.

For, you see, the Battle of the Rhododendrons was one of the many battles which had been fought, over the hills and far away, at Allways. And though I had been defeated, the thought of the fight was still sweet. It was above all a memory of innocence, of the days when one imagined that if one needed a grove of rhododendrons, all one had to do was to put them in the ground and await results. At Allways I had put them in the ground. The result after a few months had been a row of withered shrubs that looked like the remains of Christmas festivities at a seaside hotel.

'There must be something wrong with your rhododendrons,' I wrote angrily to the people who had supplied them. (Remember, this was all about nine years ago.)

'On the contrary, there must be something wrong with your soil,' they replied.

They were right, of course. It was the limiest soil in England, and lime is certain death to the rhododendron.

This discovery would have deterred any sensible person. It did not deter me. It spurred me on. I threw up everything else in the garden, and with the help of two hired boys proceeded to dig a trench so vast that it would have sheltered a large proportion of the village population in the event of an air raid. This trench was then filled with soil from a distant county where rhododendrons flourished in abundance, and planted with a fine collection of the hardiest plants I could muster. In the first year they bloomed magnificently, and I spent

53

hours bending over them, feeling — if you will not think it blasphemous — like the Creator. For I had said, 'Let there be rhododendrons,' and lo . . . there *were* rhododendrons.

But lo . . . in the following year they faded again. I had not reckoned on the rain, which had washed the poisonous lime into my beautiful trench of earth, and had shrivelled the roots as surely as if they had been burnt.

I won't go on about it, though a whole book might be written about the way in which I tried to defeat that lime; setting some plants in tubs buried in the earth, and others on little hills of special soil, far above lime level. They always died. The lime seemed to be in the very air. I had to admit defeat.

And so when Joseph suggested rhododendrons I remembered that long battle for the purple trophies which had always eluded me. I remembered, too, a walk in Ken Wood, only a mile away from Heathstead, last spring, when the whole valley was aflame with them, as though the spirit of May had lit a chain of bonfires to drive away the London mist. If they could grow them there, I could grow them here.

I turned to Joseph with a sudden enthusiasm.

'Yes,' I said, 'I'll have . . .'

I was going to say fifty. I had forgotten the squalid little triangle in which we were standing. Why — a single full-sized rhododendron would almost fill it!

I felt flat and depressed. 'I'll have three,' I said.

'Yes, sir,' Joseph agreed. 'Three'll be enough. If we get 'em small, and train 'em back, they wouldn't take up too much room.'

§ V

For the next six weeks I was away, far off in the North of England, so that I did not see the rhododendrons put in, nor any of the other things. Not that I cared very much either way. Indeed, it was only on the day of my return that I began to remember the garden at all.

To my surprise, as I drew near London I found myself thinking less unkindly about it. After the grim streets of the north, the sooty squares of the big Midland cities, even the triangle seemed not quite so harsh. Perhaps it was the perfection of the weather that induced this mood, for it was one of those days in late April when you realize that the grey face of London was silver all the time, and only needed a few spring showers and a little gentle sunshine to make it sparkle. As I drove up the long road that leads to the Heath I saw, for the first time (yes, really for the first time), all sorts of excitements in the tiny gardens which faced the road. Flowering currants, as big as those at Allways, though of course, not nearly so pink. (Or was I being unfair? *Were* they just as pink?) Forsythias, hanging their golden necklaces casually through the ancient railings. An immense double white cherry, at that ecstatic moment in its existence when the

55

sun is telling it that it cannot keep so much beauty to itself any longer, that it is high time it let the sad world gaze upon its innocence. Nothing at Allways had been more beautiful than that. Indeed, as we trundled by, and as I turned my head, for a brief moment of apostasy I wondered if there had been anything quite equal to it. For the cherry tree was silhouetted against a grimy building, that threw its snows into high relief. It looked like an *esquisse* on faded parchment by one of those anonymous Chinese artists of the sixteenth century, who had caught the spirit of an ancient spring in a few flecks of white and green.

Yes, I thought to myself, as we made our jolting, grinding, typically London-taxi progress up the hill, I really might make something pleasant out of my garden after all. Look ... there's quite a big clump of grape hyacinths over there. And that man's actually got a lawn. And that wistaria looks quite healthy. And though it's tiny that border of scillas does show that somebody's taking pains.

In fact, as at last we reached the summit, and proceeded jerkily down the road that leads to Highways Close, I actually found myself looking forward to seeing the garden again! I even had a faint regret that I hadn't put in a few more things. Still, the Siberian wallflowers ought to be quite gay. And that clump of daffodils, in the shade, might still have a few flowers left. There should be a little green on the silver birches, and the rhododendrons might have a few buds. . . .

§ V I

Five minutes later, I was sitting by the fire, with my back to the window, swearing that I would never look at that garden again. That I'd sell it. Fill it with orphan children. Wire it in and offer it to a society for lost dogs. Have it packed up in small parcels and dropped into the Atlantic Ocean.

Why this sudden change? Why this abrupt transit from spring to midwinter?

I don't know. At least, I do, but it sounds very affected and precious, and you may think me a fool. However, we'll have to risk that.

You see, it was really a question of pure aesthetics. Or perhaps you might say, of simple geometry. That triangle again. Everything that I had done . . . and it was little enough . . . had only served to emphasize its triangularity. As I stood there, in the french window, prepared to go out and make friends with the flowers, however dingy, to go through all the motions of Making the Tour, however inadequate, my eyes began to squint and my head to ache, because of the sheer hideousness of the general design.

The Siberian wallflowers at the foot of the right fence marched blatantly to join the daffodils at the foot of the left fence. One large, premature rhododendron flower sat on the apex, like a tassel on a clown's cap. And in the middle, three grimy silver birches repeated, in miniature, the horror of the triangle itself.

57

It was not to be borne.

Just as I was about to turn away, and seek the friendly refuge of the fire, a faint purr-meow echoed from below. I looked down. It was Cavalier. Very chic and glistening in his new spring coat. I lifted him up, turned him over, stroked his stomach, put his large paw on my forehead. Without putting it into words, I indicated to Cavalier that life was a sad business, and that this world was no place for the likes of us. Cavalier blinked. The sunlight shone on his green eyes, till the pupils were as narrow as caraway seeds. Slowly he turned his head towards the garden. If looks could have killed, every green thing in that triangle would have withered, so deep was his contempt.

His muscles tightened in the signal which means, in cat language, 'I desire to descend'. I obeyed the signal. I placed him on the steps that led to the 'garden'. He stood there, sniffing delicately, disdainfully. Then, he looked over his shoulder at me, and made one of those faint and tragic wails that always make me feel that one day I shall be obliged to go to Siam.

'What is it, Cavalier?'

Again he opened his mouth. But this time, the wail was so faint that one could hardly hear it. It seemed to come from ten thousand miles away.

'What is it, Cavalier? How do you feel about it?'

And then, with exquisite tact, he showed me.

He stalked across the humpy parody of a lawn, his back glistening in the sunlight. He reached the bed of

58

Siberian wallflowers. He sniffed one of the flowers, and sneezed. He looked once more over his shoulder.

And then, slowly, deliberately . . . he began to scrape.

That was how Cavalier felt about it.

And that was how I felt about it, too.

CHAPTER IV

A RAY OF LIGHT

By May the situation was so desperate that I had come to the conclusion that if the triangle could not be conquered, I should be obliged to leave the house.

These were agonizing weeks. Hundreds of sheets of paper passed from my desk into the waste-paper basket, all covered with triangles, turned upside down and inside out. Dozens of hours were spent prowling in the garden itself, like a caged hyena. But however long you prowled, nothing ever came of it. You could stand in the window and look at the apex, and stand in the apex and look at the window, and your mind remained a blank. You could stand in the middle and half close your eyes, and imagine little hedges and paths. All to no purpose. I even tried going down to the apex, bending down, and looking at the wretched thing from between my legs. But all I saw was the distant face of Mrs. Heckmondwyke looking from her window upside down. I tried to bend back again slowly and with dignity, brushing an imaginary speck of dirt from my trousers.

§ 11

Since nothing, very evidently, was going to come out of my own head, I began to buy all the gardening magazines, to see what they had to suggest. These magazines made things far worse, for two reasons. Firstly, because their advertisements (which I have never been able to resist) filled me with an agony of restlessness at the reminder of all the things I was missing. I knew, in my moments of cooler judgment, that some of those advertisements were, to say the least of it, optimistic, that the 'monstrous spikes of dazzling blossom', so glibly promised, would only prove to be a rather feeble hollyhock after all. But that didn't make it any better. One doesn't read gardening advertisements in moments of cooler judgment. One reads them in an ecstasy of unquestioning faith. That is why everybody should buy shares in seed firms.

The other reason why the gardening magazines were a drawback was because none of them, not a single one, offered the faintest hint that there might be, in this world, such a curiosity as the owner of a triangular garden at all. I was apparently a freak. A lonely, pitiable object, with no place in the scheme of things. There were Plans for square gardens, Plans for oblong gardens, and Plans for 'irregular sites' (which sounded faintly disreputable, as though they were the sort of places where suburban widows would lie in large striped hammocks, fanning themselves). But there was no Plan for a triangle.

There were Lay-Outs for long and narrow gardens. There were 'suggestions as to what can be done in a dark corner' (which again sounded faintly disreputable). There were 'informal methods of treating a pool'. There was even something about 'gaiety in the Courtyard'. But there was no Lay-Out, no suggestion, not even the faintest hint, of what you could do with a triangle.

Pentagons, yes. Hexagons, octagons in abundance. How to transform a railway-siding into the garden of Eden — by all means. How to bring beauty to the cellar, how to grow nectarines on the top of a sky-scraper, naturally. But on the method of treating a triangle — on the very existence of a triangle — a long, unbroken silence.

And all the time the agony was intensified by the fact that a golden May had given place to a flaming June, which, in its turn, was burning towards a glorious midsummer. Everything was beautiful, except the garden. You had to go up to my bedroom window if you wanted to realize how amazingly countrified we were. From this point you looked down on the great weeping willow at Number 4 — a mist of palest green — and beyond it to a series of lawns and gardens, dips and hills and little hollows, as far as you could see. Thanks to the willow, and a friendly line of poplars, hardly a house was in sight. Just a roof here and there, and a wall or two, and now and then a gabled window, half hidden in the trees.

Some of these trees were magnificent. I have never seen a finer copper beech than the one that you can see from my window. By its side are two apple trees. When they are covered in blossom, I go up to the window and look at them through a pair of binoculars. But what was the use of it all? Where was the comfort in all this beauty, if every time you looked out of the window you felt an irresistible desire to squint?

§ I I I

Then, without warning, a light dawned. In the space of ten minutes I discovered the solution, or at least the beginning of the solution, of the whole problem.

It was a sultry Sunday afternoon, early in July. I strolled out on to the terrace, and gazed with hatred at the triangle. It looked more blatant than ever. Brown, dusty, baking in the sunlight. I turned back to the house, and just as I was stepping in, I paused. After all, though the triangle was hideous, it was at least hot. One could sunbathe in it.

Why not? After all, the English sun, on the rare occasions when it appears, behaves very much like the French. That is to say, it turns the flesh pink, produces a headache, brings out blisters, and performs all the other tortures which are the necessary preliminaries to a tan. Why not go through these tortures in England, before the holidays began? Then, as one slid out of a bathing wrap on the beach, everybody would be dazzled. They would say, 'Where *did* you get that beautiful tan?' To which one would reply, 'In the garden of my London residence'. Which would mean another ten per cent on the bill, if the beach attendant were within ear-shot.

Anyway, I decided to sunbathe.

Now this is not as simple as it sounds. Apart from the fact that there is something faintly grotesque in the business of going up to a hot London bedroom, in the middle of a summer afternoon, and solemnly undressing . . . apart from the fact that the would-be sunbather feels all wrong, hitching on a bathing costume when his naked feet are standing on a carpet, and then padding down the stairs in a dressing-gown, like some peculiar animal . . . apart from the fact that he can find nothing to lie on but a hearthrug, and some silk cushions which will be ruined by being dragged about the lawn . . . apart from all these deterrents, there is the additional drawback of publicity.

Until I stepped out, almost naked, on to the terrace, I had not realized the extent to which the triangle was overlooked. True, there were various strategic points from which it was possible not to see, but there was no strategic point from which it was possible not to be seen. No — that is not quite true. There was one, immediately under the fence on the terrace outside my study window. When crouched against this fence, facing due south, with the left knee drawn up towards the chin and the neck tilted at an angle of 33 degrees, nobody could see anything except one's right ankle, unless he happened to be making a descent in a parachute immediately above.

However, this was not my idea of sunbathing. Such a position, apart from inducing cramp, would result in a striped and tigerish appearance. Many parts — essential parts, too — would remain a loathsome white.

Besides, the splinters in the back would be very hard to explain. So I got up again, aching, sweating, covered with sooty smudges, but still determined to get a tan.

It need hardly be mentioned that during all these preliminaries the window curtains at Number 1 showed signs of incessant agitation. Behind those curtains Mrs. H. was crouched, on and off, throughout the whole afternoon. However, I was too hot to bother about her.

There were two big screens in the house, and in a few minutes I had carried them out on to the lawn. The position of them — which is important to this story — was as below.

It took a little time to find exactly the right place, but in the end I discovered it. There was full sunlight, and

65

there seemed to be a reasonable amount of shelter from prying eyes.

But there was a great deal more than that. For as soon as I sat down, I found that there was complete and unbroken privacy, North, South, East and West. Of a sudden I had created a little patch of solitude in the heart of the greatest city in the world.

I could hardly believe it. I sat up. Craned my neck. Not a window, not a chimney top. I rolled over to the left, at least a yard. Still not a sign of life. I rose to my knees. Curiouser and curiouser. The neighbouring houses, even now, were completely obscured. Then, very slowly, I stood up, draping a towel cautiously round me, in case of any sudden collapse of the barricade. My heart leaped within me as I realized that all I could see was the extreme top of Mrs. H.'s roof.

I was alone. Utterly, divinely alone. Gone was the House-Next-Door, vanished were the inhabitants of Numbers 2, 3 and 4. Non-existent, apart from her roof-top, was Mrs. H. And though, as you may have guessed, I had the greyest opinion of Mrs. H., I could not believe that she would be so sunk in depravity as to wish to spend her life lying on the tiles in order to observe the slowly deepening complexion of my shoulders.

I lay down again, and grinned. For a little while I enjoyed the luxury of this strange and unexpected peace. The sky was very blue and the sunlight danced in and out of the branches of the great willow. There was such a multitude of shifting lights, so many swift sarabands of shadow, that you would say some giant and ghostly hand was poised above it, scattering confetti through the tangled boughs, confetti of gold and silver, that melted into the summer airs.

I sighed with contentment, and turned over. This was good. Very good indeed. The earth smelled of earth. Real earth, like the country. And in this part of the triangle there was more grass than I had guessed. Genuine grass, that you could pull up, and bite, and spit out again. Grass with ants on it. Orthodox ants. That climbed up the legs, and made one twitch, and sit up, and think vague, disturbing thoughts.

I sat up.

In more senses than one. For I was asking myself whether my hatred of the triangle *was* based on its triangularity? Whether the true reason might not have been that much of it was exposed to the public view? Whether — and here I looked round at the flimsy fences — if I built walls, high walls, and threw up another wall in place of these screens . . . ?

I stood up once more.

And it was precisely at this moment that my pants fell off, that the screen blew over, that the curtains at Number 1 were madly agitated and . . . and that the garden was born.

CHAPTER V

DEFEAT OF ISOSCELES

I PULLED up my pants, adjusted the screen, cast a haughty look at the curtains of Number 1, and hurried inside to ring up Mr. Peregrine.

But it was Sunday. Mr. Peregrine could not be rung up. The delay was sickening. A wall had to be built where those screens were standing, and it had to be built at once.

I wandered disconsolately back to the window, and looked out.

What?

What had happened? It wasn't possible. I looked again. But it *was* possible. It had happened. The most extraordinary thing . . . indeed, two most extraordinary things had happened. Not only was the garden, of a sudden, twice as large as it had been a moment ago, *but the triangle had almost entirely disappeared!*

It seemed like a miracle. Of course it was only an optical illusion, but what did that matter, as long as the illusion was perfect? The main reason for this remarkable change was because the screen on the left completely hid the fence behind it, so that for all you knew my garden might continue indefinitely, right up to the trees of the House-Next-Door. In terms of geometry, the change may be expressed like this:

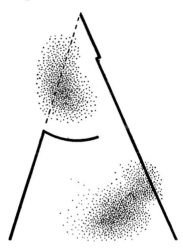

Admittedly it was still not a very pleasant shape, but it was a shape that you could do *something* with. It seemed to say, 'Come on. What are you going to do about this ugly mug of mine?'

I hurried down to the screens once more. Yes. They formed a tiny garden, all on its own, new, unexpected, full of exciting possibilities. But they did more than this. If you continued to walk to the end, turned round, and looked at the garden from the apex, the screens seemed to double the size of the whole plot from this viewpoint too, just as they had doubled it when you looked from the house.

Oh, there was no doubt about it. At last we had

something. Something over which we could plot and plan, and even dream. As I stood there, I saw how we might have a curved bed in one corner, and a couple of trees and a narrow winding path. It would be difficult enough, even now. It would demand every ounce of one's ingenuity. And though the design might be made perfect, it would still be a very tiny garden indeed. But it would be . . . a garden.

I walked back to the house, feeling that whatever the next few months might bring me, in the shape of triumph or disaster, they would not be bringing a moment's boredom.

§ 11

Before the light had faded on this momentous day I had decided that there was one thing which must be done before we could perfect the design. And that was, to replace these nasty little wooden fences by stout brick walls.

It may seem foolish, in a city of bricks, to go adding more bricks. But I felt now what I had never felt before, that something really worth while might be made out of this patch, that it might grow into a place which would demand rare creepers and exciting vines and extra-special climbing roses, and for that sort of thing the wooden fences were not good enough. Besides, apart from the fact that brick walls grow old and mellow, they are more malleable than wood. You can curve them. And it was most important that in two respects the walls should be curved. Firstly, as the ground sloped slightly downwards, they would have to be 'stepped'. The wooden fence went like this:

The wall would go like this:

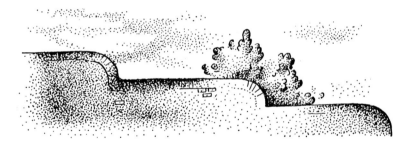

Secondly, the vital wall which I was going to build in the middle would also have to be curved. I found that out by the screens. If you put the screens in a straight line, the triangle, for some reason best known to geometricians, still worried you. It was only when you bent the screens out in a semi-circle that the triangle suffered a really serious defeat.

It was such fun, fiddling about with the screens (which were reinforced by curtains, kitchen tables turned on end, and anything we could get to simulate a wall), that it was some days before I sent for Mr. Peregrine. Perhaps it was just as well, because by these experiments I discovered that the design became even better by adding another little wall on the right-hand side, so that we would have this effect:

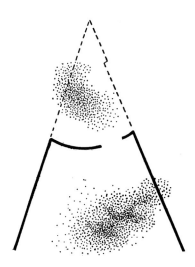

Now that was better, don't you think? Not only did it make a fresh assault on the triangle (for the two dotted lines would be completely invisible from the house) but it heightened the individuality of the little garden at the end. Why, one could even call it a 'secret' garden! It *was* secret. Once inside it, you were hidden from everybody, except such persons as might chance to find themselves on Mrs. H.'s roof.

Mrs. H.! That reminded me. Before building this wall permission must be asked from the neighbours. Those neighbours! Mysterious, unutterably remote, yet capable of casting such powerful spells, for good or evil, over our lives!

§ I I I

At first, all went well. Numbers 2 and 3 had no objection. And the Howards at Number 4 said that they would be delighted to have a wall, because it would give them a much better background for their herbaceous border. As for the lady in the House-Next-Door, she had no objection, though she ventured to hope that the workmen would deal gently with her roses, which were trained to the other side of the fence.

There remained — need I say it? — Mrs. H.

Now Mrs. H., as it happened, was the one person in the Close who had absolutely no cause to express any opinion on this matter, one way or the other. Owing to the curious way in which our gardens had been sliced out of the original land, my garden had less than one foot of common frontier with hers. But she made more fuss out of this one foot than the others had made out of their sixty feet.

'I know,' she said to me, buttonholing me in the drive

73

one morning, 'I know that you are *quite* within your rights' — I knew that too — 'I have no say in the matter. None at all.'

'What matter, Mrs. H.?'

Such innocence did not deceive Mrs. H. She did not even pretend that it did. 'Of course,' she continued, 'you are at liberty to put up a wall of corrugated iron, if you choose. It's your wall. Entirely yours.' She bared her teeth in a very menacing smile. 'Strange, our laws.' She shook her head. 'Very strange.'

'I'm afraid I don't understand.'

Another smile. 'No? Corrugated iron.'

'But I have no intention of . . .'

'Tiles, slate, pebbles — anything!' (Oh, she was very angry.)

'But I'm putting up a *brick* wall, Mrs. H.'

'Brick!' She nodded fiercely. 'So I understand. And my sweet old wooden wall has to come down.'

'It certainly hasn't to do anything of the sort, Mrs. H. Not unless you wish to pull it down yourself.'

'I do *not* wish to pull it down,' she exclaimed. 'Any more than I wish to destroy trees or turn the whole of Heathstead into a barracks.'

I tried to be patient. 'Mrs. H.,' I said, 'there are three whole gardens between yours and mine.'

'Mercifully,' she snapped.

'And the amount of your wooden wall which will adjoin my brick wall will be less than twelve inches. You needn't remove an inch of your own wall, if you don't want to do so. In fact,' I added coldly, 'I really cannot see in what way you are concerned, directly or indirectly.'

Upon which I turned to go.

She held out her hand to stop me. She gulped. She regained control of herself. She saw that I was not to be seduced from my intention, so she changed her line of attack.

'Well, well!' she exclaimed, with a heroic sigh. 'It's splendid, that we both feel so strongly about our little gardens. Splendid! Nothing like keenness. Nothing! Competition! Splendid!' (She sounded as if she were addressing a group of exceptionally energetic girl guides.) 'So now we know where we stand.'

She paused. Another sigh. 'My clematis. Do you think you could spare my clematis?'

'But as far as I remember, it's at the other end of the wall.'

'At the moment, yes. But things grow very quickly in Heathstead. Wonderful soil. And that reminds me . . . if you *could* keep the building-lime away from the azaleas?'

'But they're right on the other side of the garden!'

'Quite. But workmen have a way of straying.'

'I don't think they could get through the gap in the fence. If they came into your garden at all, they'd have to climb over the wall.'

'Oh dear! Will they be doing *that*?'

'I can't think of any reason why they should wish to

do so,' I replied sharply, for the conversation was beginning to bore me. I looked her straight in the eyes, and repeated, 'I can think of *no* reason why any workman should wish to go anywhere near your garden.'

We glared at each other. Oh dear, this was terrible. Such hatred! Such implacable contempt!

'Well,' she hissed, 'that, I suppose, is that.'

'Yes,' I hissed back. 'It is.'

We both turned sharply, and retired to our respective abodes, I to narrate the whole episode to Cavalier, and she to pour out her troubles to her Ada. I hope that she had a better audience than I had. For it was fish day, and Cavalier's attention on such occasions is inclined to wander.

§ I V

Do you mind pausing for a moment? It occurs to me that the bitterness which always marred my encounters with Mrs. H. may leave a nasty taste in your mouth, may make you think of me as a most unneighbourly kind of person. It isn't really quite as bad as that. There are great lessons to be learned from neighbours, great riches to be garnered from them too.

For instance, in our little Close we all get the benefit of the great weeping-willow at Number 4. The pale, almost shrill green of its earliest shoots is our first sign of spring. And in autumn each little terrace is strewn with the same golden leaves. The common heritage of this lovely tree ought to have bound us together, to have given a sort of unity to our lives. Unfortunately it was not so. Beautiful things, as we have seen, do not always bind people together; they frequently tear them apart.

But there are exceptions. There are times when we do share. And then you realize that a good neighbour is a very precious thing. Consider the case of the Howards' clematis next door. It was the old-fashioned *Clematis montana*, and though it was only three years old it had flourished so wonderfully that it had already reached their roof and was throwing its tendrils, thickly starred with blossoms, against my walls. The Howards wrote me a note, suggesting that I might like to adopt these tendrils and train them over my own house. Needless to say I accepted with alacrity. There were nearly a dozen sturdy shoots, which have raced ahead so swiftly that some of them are already beginning to peer into my bedroom window.

Do you like flowers looking in at the windows? I take an almost absurd delight in such things. I never see the blossoms of the Howards' clematis — so near that I can lean out and touch them — without being reminded of the tremendous reserves of human kindness with which the world is stored. And apart from the clematis, I have my own wistaria, which has grown so fast that one day I shall be able to share it with them too. It has grown right round the window, and in summer, if you want to shut the window, you have to take great care to push away the stem, for the leaves have pushed themselves over the ledge. I feel rather guilty at shutting out so beautiful a thing, when it is obviously anxious to come inside. But it is possible that Gaskin might not like wistaria trailing over the dressing-table and on to the carpet and eventually, I suppose, into the bed. So every summer the wisteria has to be gently told that it has come far enough.

§ v

We have paused long enough. We must get back to the garden.

We need not hover about the workmen while they are building the walls. Needless to say, I hovered a great deal myself, causing delay and distraction, and sometimes having a wall built and knocked down again several times before I was satisfied. For those walls had to be right within a couple of inches, not only in their height, and their position, but in their degree of curve.

However, we got what we wanted in the end. And by the third week in September, the last brick had been laid, and the last lorry had rumbled away.

Mrs. H., meeting me in the drive, observed with a sigh that the character of Heathstead was changing very rapidly.

'Really, Mrs. Heckmondwyke? In what way?'

'It used to be like living in the country. But now . . .' Her eyes rested on a small pile of bricks which the men had left behind. She hastily averted them. She was the soul of tact, as you will have observed. All the same, she allowed herself to shake her head, and murmur:

'Quite a built-up area.' Which was, as they say, a nasty one.

For there was a certain sting of truth in her remark. If you had gone out into the garden at this period, you would have seen nothing but brick walls and a great deal of trampled clay, on which not a blade of grass was growing. There was no sign of a garden. And though there was at last a frame for a garden, even the frame was not complete.

The triangle was not yet entirely conquered. The eye was still apt to wander, with disconcerting frequency, to the right-hand wall. And the nasty little apex was still there, a perpetual thorn of irritation.

A plan will make it plain. Or will it? Let's see.

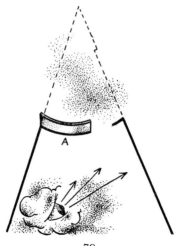

Perhaps it does not make it so very plain, after all. But the thing in the left-hand corner is the Eye, and the things coming out of it are arrows, indicating that the Eye is still being dragged over to the right.

Perhaps it would have been better to have no plan at all, because it really looks as if I had done nothing except put a curved wall across, with a gap in the middle. Actually it was far subtler than that, because, as we have seen before, the centre wall (marked A) was built just high enough to hide the wall on the left, behind it. So, for all you knew, there might be acres and acres of garden through that little gap.

But still the Eye continued to swerve to the right. (By the way, it is printed with a capital E because it is Everybody's Eye. Not only mine or yours, but all Mankind's.)

Of course, the simplest way of bringing over the Eye to the left would have been to affix sensational placards on to the left-hand wall, which would have compelled one's attention. 'Cet animal est dangereux' would have served the purpose very well. But it would not have been in keeping with the general scheme. Another way would have been to lurk behind people whenever they stepped out on to the terrace, seize them by the neck, and force them to look in the required direction. The disadvantages of this method are too obvious to enumerate. And if large scarlet arrows were painted on the terrace, like traffic signals, one would very soon tire of them.

So once again it was necessary to go slithering about over the clay, with half-closed eyes, making scooping movements with my hands, trying to find inspiration. This time it came quickly. For in order to see what was wanted, I purchased a long piece of white rope, which was laid on the clay. And after about an hour, I was quite sure that it was in the right position.

I stepped back on to the terrace. Yes. There was no question about it. The Eye followed that rope with the eagerness of a retriever on a hot scent. It never strayed for a second to the right-hand wall. It kept strictly to the trail of rope. And in doing so, it made the whole composition fall into line. With the exception of the apex, the triangle had almost ceased to exist. I say 'almost', because there were a few minor skirmishes still to come. But they will only be described in so far as they led to other excitements, unconcerned with geometry.

Now, how was that line to be introduced into the general design? The rope couldn't stay there for ever. One might change it for a hose pipe, perhaps? And leave it perpetually on the lawn, negligently, as it were? But no! That would look idiotic. Besides, it would rot. What *could* that line be?

And then, I cursed myself for being so dense. Obviously it would be a path! Not so wide, maybe, as another path I had known, nor so long, nor leading to the same adventures. But a garden path, all the same.

At last, the Eye looked almost straight ahead.

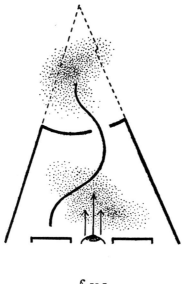

§ vi

It was with the discovery of the garden path that the drama began to move swiftly. Far too swiftly, indeed, for Mrs. H. On the very next morning (the day after she had made the remark about the built-up area) — yet another lorryload of bricks descended upon her. When I say 'descended' I mean it almost literally. They had been so hurriedly stacked that when the lorry drew up, they crashed to the ground with a noise like a major bombardment, just as she was going out for a walk.

You see, I had decided for several reasons that the path must be made of brick. Firstly, because the line of

82

it was so vital to the general design that it would have been dangerous to experiment with anything else. Secondly, because in such a small garden you had to make the path scrupulously neat and tidy, and it was easier to do that with brick than with gravel or clay. Thirdly, because by a curious paradox, if you had used anything but brick, the walls would have looked even brickier.

No sooner had the path been laid down (in imagination) than a whole host of fascinating ideas presented themselves. For example, would it not be possible to make it narrower as it receded from the house, tapering it in order to give the illusion of perspective? Yes — it would be possible. In fact, when we came to lay it down, we tried it out. But it looked a little ridiculous. If your garden path is only four bricks wide, and if — by an error of judgment — you have not adopted the career of a tightrope walker, you will find that any attempt to modify the dimensions of those four bricks will end, quite simply, in your walking on the grass.

But there was another idea, which we did adopt. And that was to give the path two quite separate characters. The brick part of it finished just beyond the curve, at the centre wall. Then it stopped, and was replaced by grey stones, laid in the grass. These stones conducted, by the longest possible route, to the apex.

Needless to say, a certain amount of pedestrian technique was needed in the negotiation of such a path. The Eye could not wander quite so carelessly as it might have wished, or the feet would have strayed far away. And as soon as the curve was reached, and the secret garden entered, the feet had to be lifted very high, and short, staccato steps were the order of the day.

§ VII

Now when a thing is perfect, it meets all sorts of tests to which you had never thought of subjecting it. One of the reasons why I was sure that my path was perfect was because it met the supremely important test of making you walk the longest way round.

Does that strike an answering chord in the hearts of my fellow gardeners? If not, I must be a freak. For surely, whenever you are showing people over a garden, it is vital that they should go the longest possible way round? It may be that there is only one thing in the garden . . . say a forsythia . . . that can lay any claim to excellence, and that this forsythia can be plainly observed by even the most short-sighted, tossing its golden stars at the bottom of the lawn and demanding immediate attention.

But it must not receive attention till the right moment. There must be a conspiracy of silence about it. If some tiresome guest, stepping out on to the terrace, observes the forsythia, exclaims with delight, and proceeds to make a bee-line for it, she must be gently but firmly dragged back. People who are being shown over a garden must not behave like that. They are as rude as nasty little children at a school treat who reach for doughnuts before they have suffered the necessary martyrdom of bread and butter.

The way to the forsythia is arduous and complicated. It may lie due south, but first you must turn sharp west, and scrape behind a holly-bush ('which was a blaze in December'), and make straight for a blank wall, when lo and behold, you switch east, pausing to note the site of the proposed sundial, after which you scrape by the hollybush again (in front this time) and make straight for another wall ('where, if you could only see it in June, the wistaria is *not* to be believed'), and then you walk down a very twisting path which turns back to the holly-bush just as it seems to be leading to the forsythia . . . and so on. All the time, you must be unaware of the forsythia. To look at it too soon is not only impolite. It is positively cruel.

My design passed this test with flying colours. Unless I had led people round and round in circles, it would have been impossible for them to take longer in walking from the front window to the apex of the triangle.

CHAPTER VI

BIRTH OF A BUBBLE

But when they got to the apex . . . what then?

Life is meaningless without some aim, and so is a garden path. By which I do not mean that you have to have some awful little statue glowering at you from the end, or some unnecessary sundial, or a door leading nowhere. All I mean is that if you are walking down the garden path you must walk to *something*, even if it is only a tree, or a gap in the hedge through which you can look out on to quiet fields. To put it on the lowest level, it gives you something to say, such as, 'Well, here we are!' Or . . . more fancifully . . . 'The leaves are beginning to fall, what?' Or, if your friend is not interested in gardens, you can direct his attention through the gap in the hedge and say, 'Look, there is a cow'. (You need not look at it yourself.)

But I had no tree, no hedge, no fields, and my nearest approach to a cow was Mrs. H. All I had was a triangular apex, built of brick. Indeed, as we saw on page 51, it was not even a strictly triangular apex. You will remember that this odd shape was due to the difficulty experienced by the architect of the Close when trying to slice five gardens out of a space which had previously held only one.

It was nice to have that extra bit in the top right-hand corner, but it did not make the task of dealing with it any easier. It seemed that the only thing to do with it was to fill it up, once again, with rhododendrons. (The original rhododendrons, needless to say, had long since departed.) However, one would have to be feeling particularly bright to find anything new to say about three small rhododendrons, after the hundredth visitor had been shown down the garden path. Besides, rhododendrons, beautiful as they are in flower, are not the sort of thing that one wants to gaze at, month after month.

I stood in front of that apex, pondering. The wall on the right was only half up. The sunlight poured in from the garden of the House-Next-Door. It was a regular sun-trap, that apex. When the wall was up, of course, it wouldn't get any sun at all. But . . . *but why build the wall?* I suddenly asked myself. Why shut out this precious sunlight? Here is the one place for the 'feature' you have been looking for, the climax, the object, the end of the path . . . a greenhouse!

§11

The enthusiasm engendered by this inspiration was subjected, during the next few days, to some rude shocks.

First, it appeared that there was a thing called 'Ancient Lights'. If I had not had personal acquaintance with it,

I should have presumed it to have been the favourite institution of the great family of Tite Barnacle. It bore the hall-mark of the Circumlocution Office firmly stamped on every feature. For here was the ridiculous situation. If I built a wall, and inserted a window in it, I should be violating the sacred principle of Ancient Lights. Not — I hasten to add — in the direction of the neighbours *behind*, but in the direction of the House-Next-Door, on to whose garden the window would look.

On the other hand — and this is the idiotic part — if I built no wall (and hence, as is obvious, no window), I should not be violating anything at all. I could leave that great gap open, and if I chose, I could sit in it all day, making such awful faces at the Lady-Next-Door that her garden would be a misery to her, but she would not be able to do anything about it.

Build a wall with a window, and you are unwarrantably overlooking your neighbour, said Ancient Lights. Build no wall at all, stand in the gap and glare at your neighbour all day, and you are *not* guilty of overlooking your neighbour, they added.

Well, fortunately the Lady-Next-Door, who was the only person concerned besides myself, must have seen how ridiculous this was. For she raised no objections, and only expressed the faint hope that whatever activity might be imminent on the Western Front should be achieved as quickly as possible, because her flower-beds were beginning to feel the strain.

After the Ancient Lights had been properly put in their place, a whole host of other difficulties presented themselves. I am a practical gardener, and though it is pleasant to wander about paying homage to beautiful things, it is also necessary to pay homage to ugly things, such as drains. The drainage of the greenhouse was a real problem. The obvious place for an outlet was into the garden of the House-Next-Door, but I did not even contemplate that, partly out of common politeness, and partly because I had an awful suspicion that somewhere in the laws of England there must be a thing called Ancient Waters, and it would be too depressing to go into all that again.

Eventually we solved it by two large drainage pits, cunningly arranged beneath the lawn of the secret garden. There were several minor worries connected with the digging of these pits, but there is not time to tell you about them. For the main problem, the shape of the greenhouse itself, was looming larger and larger on the horizon.

After all, it was to be a 'feature'. It had to be beautiful in itself. And it had to be an integral part of the general design, completing it, crowning it.

This was going to be a long job, so I went out and bought a camp stool, transported it to the secret garden, sat down behind the wall, and waited for inspiration. It was a happy pastime, because in this position one was completely hidden from the world, and could make faces, wave hands and squint through fingers, without any danger of being over-looked. Also, London was basking in a long stretch of glorious weather. An anti-cyclone was permanently clamped on the map of England.

I was really enjoying all the sensations that children must enjoy with a new and very superior box of bricks. The bricks were actually there, stacked at the side.

Yes, it was great fun.

But after spending some days in the luxury of gloating, it became time to get a move on. I was not sitting here for nothing. Nor convalescing from a disease of the lungs. I was trying to see how to create, in the corner, a green-house which would not be too hideous.

I put down on a piece of paper the things which *had* to happen, whether I liked it or not (or whether anybody else liked it or not, which was probably more important). The first was, that since the greater part of the light would have to come from the south-west — i.e. across the lawn of the House-Next-Door — the wall on the right must not be more than about two feet high. The rest must be nothing but glass.

The second necessity was that the front of the green-house would have to be curved. It was extraordinary, how these curves dictated themselves, time and again, when the garden was being designed.

With these two necessities, for the time being, I had to be content. Mr. Peregrine was summoned, shown what was required, and asked to produce a sketch. After a few days, he brought something like this:

It looked rather too much like a tent for my liking. Also, the glass roof would be plainly visible from my bedroom window, and that roof would be triangular. The sun would shine on it by day and the moon would go down on it by night — or should one say go up? — but whichever one should say, my spirit would be sore distressed. So Mr. Peregrine went away and left me to brood.

§III

Then, once again, life intervened, in the person of a Mr. Sprott, insurance agent. And the problem, in a few magic seconds, was solved.

It happened like this. From time to time, in spite of the most admirable secretarial arrangements, all the insurance policies in my house are lost. It is a phenomenon against which no powers of foresight or ingenuity seem to be effective. I say to myself, 'Where are those insurance policies?' and rush upstairs, and nobody knows. We ring up solicitors, banks, chartered accountants. Nobody has them. They always turn up in a day or two, but in the meantime Gaskin is asked to be more than usually careful not to burn down the house, and who was that strange-looking man selling bootlaces last week?

Well, Mr. Sprott came along one afternoon during such a crisis, because it really was necessary to clear up this idiotic situation. And while he was having a cup of tea, I told him that we were building a greenhouse, and asked him if it could be insured.

'Not against war,' said Mr. Sprott, sharply.

Somehow it had not occurred to me to insure against war. If the skies were ever black with General Goering's young heroes, even the fact that one was underwritten at Lloyds would be of small comfort.

'Hailstorms, naturally,' continued Mr. Sprott. 'Children? Stones?'

Stones! Mrs. H., undoubtedly, would be only too delighted to hurl stones at the greenhouse. But there was no need to tell Mr. Sprott that. Mrs. H. was the sort of person whom Lloyds would have to take in their stride. So he was informed that there were no children, and the stones . . . as you might say . . . were 'waived'.

'In that case,' said Mr. Sprott, 'there should be no difficulty. I'll make you out a policy, if you like. Quite inexpensive.' He paused, and added, in tones which somehow sounded very significant, 'Unless, of course, you were having a dome?'

'A dome!'

I smiled. What should I want with a dome? This was to be a greenhouse, not a mosque. But the smile faded as quickly as it had come. For my mind's eye had suddenly seen a picture of the dome as it would look when it was completed, and my mind's eye liked it very much indeed.

Meanwhile Mr. Sprott was continuing to dilate on the comparative expensiveness of insuring domes. He was a persuasive little man, and though I was only half listening to him, I gained a vague impression that domes would automatically draw down lightning from a cloudless sky, and act as a magnet to any small boys in the neighbourhood, filling their hearts with evil thoughts. But as I said, I was only half listening to him. For the dome was taking shape, all the time, in my head.

If it was exactly the right size, it would round off the garden in a manner which could be achieved by no other method. The last hateful scrap of the triangle would disappear. Instead, there would be a silver bubble floating against a background of green. If there were ever snow, it would look like a beautiful boiled egg. If there was a fog, you could put a light in the top and it would guide your weary feet down the path. Oh, but yes

93

— beyond the shadow of a doubt, there must be a dome.

I interrupted Mr. Sprott. 'As a matter of fact, I *had* been thinking of a dome.'

Mr. Sprott sniffed. He evidently thought that he might have been told that before. However, he merely said, 'In that case, you'll have to have Policy 173B', or words to that effect.

After which, he departed.

§ I V

A week later, Mr. Peregrine was there, dome in hand. Or rather, a picture of it, designed by his favourite architect from a drawing I had made myself.

Any doubts which there may have been about the general desirability of domes were instantly dispelled by that drawing. It was not quite like the dome which you see in the photograph. It was more sumptuous; it suggested rather more forcibly that Marie Antoinette was inside it, doing something lurid. But when it had been toned down, it was nearer perfection than I had dared to hope.

Don't you honestly think so too? Could you really have arrived at anything better? Before you say 'Yes', glance back at that other photograph, showing 'As it was in the Beginning'. Refresh your mind with the sharp edges of that triangle. Recall how tiny the whole thing

was. Well — now it doesn't seem tiny. Now the triangle has disappeared. And now . . . but I can't go on blowing my own trumpet like this.

It was not only, nor even principally, for the elegance of its exterior that the dome was such a godsend. The extra height would mean that the inside of the house could shelter a far wider range of plants than would be possible under a flat roof. On examining the plans accompanying the drawing, I was astonished at the amount of space that would be available. That little extra bit in the corner made all the difference. I shuddered to recall how nearly it had been given to Mrs. H.

Why, there was no end to the things we could grow there! For instance, at long last I should be able to satisfy my ambition to have a bougainvillaea, that lovely purple creeper that looks as if Nature had designed it specially to hang out for Coronations, royal processions, and occasions of great pomp and ceremony. Perhaps there might even be three bougainvillaeas, the scarlet and the rose as well as the purple? But no, because then there would be no room for a mimosa, and one *had* to have a mimosa. A mimosa will flourish and grow as large as you like; in quite a small tub (I know one which has been in the same tub for more than thirty years). And one of the advantages of mimosa grown under glass in a temperate house such as mine would be, is that it lasts a good two weeks if you cut it and bring it indoors. The mimosa which comes from the south of France always

95

seems to shrivel up, and looks very parched and miserable after the first twenty-four hours.

I couldn't wait. The wretched Mr. Peregrine was harried night and day. Domes, it appeared, had to be specially made. They required the attention of expert technicians. New moulds would have to be cast, and the glass must be cut with particular care. From the way he went on, you would think that I was acting as a serious hindrance to Britain's Great Rearmament Effort, that men were being dragged away from digging air-raid shelters in order to pander to a morbid taste for flowers. Shameful to say, I was in such a state of eagerness that I should not much have cared if this had been the case. If nobody is ever going to build another greenhouse just because of Hitler, then we might as well go out into the garden right away, and not only eat worms, but do our best to imitate them in all other respects.

Here in the greenhouse I should at last be able to meet the countryman on his own ground, with equal weapons. Indeed, in some ways, I should be better equipped. Much as you may love your greenhouse in the country, you must honestly admit that there are a good many winter nights when it is with considerable reluctance that you rise from a comfortable fireside, wrap up against the cold and rain, and stumble down the path, to grope about among a lot of clinkers by the light of a torch. Four times out of five, maybe, it is fun. But on the fifth, the fire is out, and won't get lit again, and you have to slither all the way back to the house for a chunk of live coal, and you fall down and twist your ankle, and say a number of sharp things. And meanwhile the plants are slowly being chilled to death. The city dweller need have none of these picturesque but over-rated ardours. All he has to do is to press an electric switch . . . and there is a tale to tell you about *that*, before the night is out.

The very contrast, too, between the grime outside (though London grime is much exaggerated) and the spotless cleanliness inside the house is refreshing. 'But you've got to have ventilation,' you may say. 'Doesn't the soot get in?' No, it doesn't. Or rather, it needn't. Of course, if you leave the doors and windows wide open during a fog, soot might get in. So, for that matter, might an elephant. But there are ways and means of ventilating a greenhouse without allowing a particle of soot to get in. It is a rather technical business, so I will not trouble you with it.

However, there is one technicality which should be mentioned (As it is for gardeners only, please skip to p. 102 if you are not interested.)

I had decided that as it would be so simple to obtain heat in the city, I should have a temperate house, with a minimum winter temperature of about 55 degrees. This would allow of a very wide range of semi-tropical plants and would not be too hot for a number of hardier things. This heat would be obtained by electricity — it meant knocking down walls, digging up drains, and heaven knows what, in order to get the electric cable from the house to the greenhouse, but we were getting used to that by now.

A friend had told me about a little electric heater that was thermostatically controlled. So one was bought, and during the early autumn it seemed to work very well. (We are anticipating things a little, but you must forgive that.)

Then, one day, without any warning, a wave of intense cold swept over Britain. In the early morning it had been almost balmy, but at noon the temperature dropped precipitately, the sky became a sheet of grey, frozen steel, and by four o'clock it was just too cold to be funny.

I had been out to lunch, and on reaching home the first thing I did was to run out to the greenhouse. Consternation! Although the little machine was whirring merrily away, and although it was set, as usual, at 55, the temperature had dropped to 48. I set the dial to 65, and went in to have an uneasy cup of tea. Half an hour later, with real alarm, I discovered that in spite of altering the dial, the temperature had gone down to 40. There was no time to be lost. Everybody, for some reason, was out. I scrambled into the car, and sped to the nearest ironmonger's, to buy an oil-stove. In the entrance I collided with a large woman in a fur coat. On her face was a look of triumph, and in her hand was an oil-stove. The last in the shop! 'Never had such a run on them,' said the ironmonger, who was an evil-looking man.

To another ironmonger's — the same story! To yet

another, far away. Here, at last, I managed to buy a small second-hand oil-stove, which looked as if it hadn't been lit since grandmamma aired her bustle over it. I shot back to the house, breaking all the traffic rules. The cold was incredible. Down to the greenhouse again — the thermometer registered 35! Three degrees off freezing point. And the greenhouse had only just been stocked with a marvellous collection of ... well, never mind what it was stocked with.

I poured in the paraffin with fingers that trembled, partly from cold and partly from anxiety. Turned up the wick. A dense cloud of smoke ascended. Turned down the wick again. Out went the stove. This happened three times. At last the thing began to burn properly, but it seemed to throw out very little heat.

In desperation, I ran into the house, and got a box of candles. Anything to keep the temperature up. If the worst came to the worst I would kidnap Mrs. H. and lock her in the greenhouse for the night. Nothing would freeze while *she* was in there. I sped down with the candles, and lit all twelve. Looking back on this hideous episode, I remember that they were very pretty, burning against the delicate foliage. Through the glass they made the greenhouse look like a little shrine.

Whether it was the candles or the stove or the sheer heat of my own anxiety that did the trick, it would be hard to say. But the temperature began to climb again. In half an hour it had gone back to 40. In an hour it had reached a rather precarious 42.

Meanwhile it was getting colder and colder outside, and the candles were burning away all too rapidly. So — to cut a long story short — we got hold of an old pierced bucket, and filled it with redhot coke, and rushed it down. The temperature promptly went up to 60. (Those poor plants!) By midnight it was down to 43 again, so we repeated the process. And Gaskin, who certainly deserved a medal, promised to set his alarum clock, and get up at 4 a.m. in order to replenish the brazier once again.

On the following morning we bought another oil-stove, which functioned much better, and on the day after that the cold spell broke. However, I had learned my lesson. Not only were the plants blackened with oily fumes, which took days to wash off, but the whole household was in a state of nervous exhaustion. Even the cats were slightly hysterical, and had to be calmed down with quantities of fresh haddock.

So Mr. Peregrine came up again, and set things to rights. He put in three big electric plates which were concealed under the shelves. Don't ask me what they are. I have no idea. All I know is that they work perfectly. You simply set them at 55, and the thermo-static control sees to it that the temperature remains at that level. I don't want to say anything against that other machine. It did its best, but it was not strong enough to withstand the rigours of the English climate.

Well, the moral of all this is that if you are heating your greenhouse electrically, do, for goodness sake, try it out on a really cold day *before* you put your plants in.

However, this story belongs to the future. We must retrace our steps, to the days when the greenhouse was still only a dream on paper. We have had enough of bricks. It is high time that we began to think of flowers.

CHAPTER VII

ENTER FLORA

WHERE are we? October, is it not? The main walls are up, and the path is laid. The general design, in fact, is at last complete. And, as I said before, it is high time that we began to think about flowers.

Flowers? What sort of flowers? No — it is still too soon to ask that question. There is another that is even more urgent — where are the flowers to be put?

In case that sounds obscure, let me explain more fully.

If you had stood on the terrace, at this period, you would have realized a very important and very disturbing thing. Namely, that the one place where flowers *ought* to have been planted was the only spot where they could *not* be planted. The obvious position for a border was against the wall on the right, because this wall faced south and received the full blessing of the sun. But the moment you called attention to this wall — and you would certainly call attention to it if you planted flowers there — the moment you made the Eye wander over to the right, the whole design of the garden fell to pieces. The triangle — which we had been fighting for nearly a year — was instantly reborn.

Thinking that I might have become morbidly sensitive to triangularity, I called in Joseph. There was nothing in the least morbid about *him*.

'Where do you think we ought to have the main herbaceous border, Joseph?'

'Why — over there, of course,' answered Joseph, pointing to the right-hand wall.

'All the same, Joseph, I'd like to test it first. Just to see what it looks like. So if you'll come along with me . . .'

He came along. We got a couple of spades and dug a border all down the wall. By the time we'd finished, lunch was ready. I ate it in a great hurry, snatched a hat, jumped into the car and drove to the florist's at the bottom of the hill. There I bought a number of pot plants, cheap chrysanthemums, daisies and the like — enough to give an illusion of a border. I loaded them into the car and sped back again. In twenty minutes all the pots had been sunk in the ground which had been dug along the wall. Needless to say, the effect was not artistic, but it did at least give you a faint idea of what a border would be like in that position. And it was like nothing on earth. It made the whole garden look as if it had been designed for the especial delectation of Isosceles.

Joseph returned. He blinked, and scratched his head. I explained what I had been doing, omitting any mention of the triangle.

'Something wrong,' muttered Joseph.

'Yes, but *what*?'

He folded his arms and stared, first at the right-hand wall, then at the left. He shook his head.

'Something wrong,' he repeated. Then a light dawned on him. 'Darned if that old triangle hasn't come back again!'

So I had been right. It hadn't been morbid sensitivity. For if Joseph is morbidly sensitive, Stalin is a woodland violet.

§11

Once more we began by doing the secondary things first, in the hope that the inspiration for the rest would follow. The main design, you may remember, was as shown on page 82.

A week later, it had become

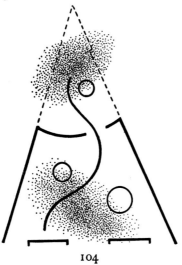

If you are bad at maps, this little plan will mean nothing. But it is really very simple. It merely shows the creation of three small circular beds, two in the front garden, and one in the secret garden. They had to be in this position, they had to be circular, and they had to be exactly the size they are. Three inches larger or smaller, and they would have looked ridiculous. As it was, they looked delightful.

The two oblongs at the base of the triangle represent the creation of two other little beds, one beneath the window of the study, and the other beneath the window of the dining-room. We had to tear up part of the terrace to make them. These beds, it was decided, were to be herbaceous. But they were also ... let's face it ... so small, so dry, and so generally inadequate, that the idea of creating an herbaceous border in them was like arranging for an Imperial honeymoon to be consummated in a hammock.

Nevertheless, the three little circular beds were just right. That was some consolation. The farthest bed, in the secret garden, was particularly successful. It was made a little smaller than the others, to give the illusion of perspective, and it was so placed that from the terrace you could only see a fraction of it. For all you knew, it might be the first of many beds, by the side of which you could wander for miles.

§III

But the creation of these beds only added to my unrest. It was such fun to dig them deep, to sift great piles of coarse earth, to pick out bits of tin and glass and rubble, to cart away the rubbish and then to scoop the new earth back again into the beds, sweetened with leaf-mould and bone-meal . . . it was such fun to do all these things, to get thoroughly filthy again, that my desire for herbaceous borders began to amount to an obsession.

For beds aren't borders, if you know what I mean. 'Planting out' can't compare in interest with the slow growth, year after year, of herbaceous stuff. The whole essence of a garden is that it becomes an old friend, or rather, a host of old friends. Will the irises be as good this year as they were last? How well will the delphiniums have stood being divided? Will the phloxes have 'established themselves' in the coming summer? These are the things that matter, that really move the heart. And though it is an endless delight to plan beds of spring and summer annuals . . . (shall it be wall-flowers or forget-me-nots, stocks or petunias?) . . . there is always a temporary feeling about such things. Almost before the wallflowers are in bloom it is time to think of their successors. You are on with the new love when the old has barely begun.

So the search was on again. I'll cut out all the pre-liminaries and give you the ultimate solution. Here it is, in another of those dreary plans:

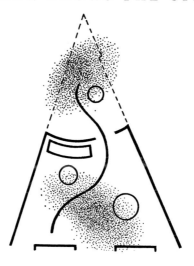

To which you might well retort: 'Why didn't you think of that before?'

The reason was simple. I never thought of it before because the left part of the border never got any sun at all, the middle got about two hours, and only the right end was ever moderately sunny. And since it is not customary to grow flowers in perpetual darkness, the idea had not presented itself to me. That was the reason, and please do not speak so brusquely to me in future.

But seriously, it seemed to be the only place, and so I had to make the best of it. I had to think of shade plants — of irises and Christmas roses, of foxgloves, polyanthus, montbretias, and lilies-of-the-valley. If only it had been a question of finding flowering *shrubs*, it would have been easy enough. One could have made a list a yard long of fuchsias, lilacs, mock-oranges, hypericums, ribes, azaleas, forsythias, guelder-roses ... but why go on? The number of flowering shrubs which seem to delight in illuminating the shadows is almost interminable. But there was room for very few shrubs; I had to concentrate on plants. And that wasn't so easy.

However, this was what happened in the end. If you are not really mad about gardening, the next page or two will bore you to tears, and you had better turn quickly to section v, where there is a bit more action.

In the dark left-hand corner I planted two very compact lilacs, pale mauve and purple. They were not young trees; they had been in a London nursery for over five years, in tubs, and they seemed to thrive on city air. They were about five feet high, so that the top of the branches got a fair amount of sun, which is essential for the flowers, though not for the roots.

In front of the lilacs, slightly to the right, I planted a generous clump of foxgloves. For several reasons. Firstly because foxgloves love shade. Secondly because they also like London ... though, heaven knows, there is no flower that so sweetly conjures up the heart of the country, as if by a magic wand, filling the mind with cool, green memories, of coppices where the bracken is waist high, of the edges of remote woods, where the rabbits so seldom see an intruder that they study you calmly and curiously before they deign to amble away.

And the third reason for the foxgloves was because although they are really biennials, they seed themselves so generously that a clump will go on for ever.

To the right of the foxgloves, at the back, I put a group of tall irises, choosing the paler blues and mauves and purples. The darker irises are very beautiful, but they wouldn't show up in that obscurity. In front of these a little space was left, to be filled either by bulbs or annuals, or something very special. But in the middle, where the sun began, I made a splash with lilies. Madonnas at the back, *regale* in the centre, and tigers to the fore. Lilies seem to love the city — in fact, one of the finest clumps of orange lily (*Lileum crocem*) which I ever saw was flowering in a back yard in Chicago.

Behind the lilies I planted a *Clematis Jackmanii*, to climb the wall. It would have been pleasant to have a rarer variety, but I wanted to be sure of success. And judging from the squalid, sooty places all over London in which it may be seen rioting away, it was fairly certain the *Jackmanii* would grow in anything, with the possible exception of a submarine.

Now for the right-hand part of the border, which got all the sun. It was very important indeed to have something outstanding here. As far as the Eye was concerned it was dead centre. That meant that the flowers which were planted at this spot would really set the tone of the garden throughout the whole summer.

Of course, there had to be some delphiniums. Life could hardly be said to be complete without them.

Whereby hangs a tale. Oh, well — perhaps it isn't a real tale, but it's something that is pleasant to talk about.

There should have been another space here — the delphiniums forbade it. There was only room for three, but that was better than nothing.

After that, I took a risk, and planted the whole remaining space — (a vast area of three feet by two!) — with phloxes, in the most brilliant shades of scarlet, salmon-pink, and crimson. I would have liked to include the deep purple Mahdi, and it was sad that there could be none of the whites, but in such a small space it was essential to get as many reds as possible, or they would have begun to pick quarrels. Two reds always fight; a dozen are always friends. It seems that the League of Flowers is the only league that really works.

Admittedly this doesn't seem very much, even for ten feet — lilac, foxgloves, irises, clematis, lilies, delphiniums, phlox. But you must not forget that space had been left in between for other things. Besides, after all it was *not* the only herbaceous border. Three more were on their way!

§ I V

But before hearing about them, please look at the photograph of the finished garden. There, behind the wall, just peeping over, you will see the top of a tree.

It concerns that old Eye again — the Eye that we always have to bring round to the left.

Which of Blake's drawings is it, that centres round an Eye? You must know it. It is very typical Blake. It shows the largest Eye you have ever seen, with wild clouds rolling round it, and a lot of naked old men frisking about in the clouds as though they were returning from a very peculiar Rotarian celebration.

Anyway, the tree is the direct result of the Eye.

It occurred to me that if only there could be a splash of colour on the *other* side of the wall, high up in that left-hand corner, the size of the garden would seem greatly enhanced. If the colour could be offset by a solid mass of green, so much the better. But how this was to be obtained, I had no idea.

Then one day I went a walk over Hampstead Heath to Golder's Green. It was early March, and the winter had been very mild. I wandered along, sniffing the air appreciatively. I strolled into the public gardens, and suddenly saw in the distance something that looked like a house on fire. It *was* a house, and it *was* on fire — with camellias. From the gravel path to the bedroom windows they blazed, twenty feet up, painting the walls pink and white and coral. It was like an old-fashioned transformation scene.

Until that moment I had shared the old, evil illusion that the camellia is a fragile, ultra-feminine flower, wilting at the least touch of frost. I had put it on the same level as those women who give sepulchral coughs if their wraps slide off their shoulders, for even a moment, at gala nights on the *Côte d'Azur*. Why, even in so alarmingly omniscient a work as Mr. Montagu Free's *Gardening*, which has done more to humanize the United States than any of the most painstaking reformers, you will find the wicked statement that the camellia requires not only a peaty soil (which is 'all my eye and Betty Martin') but *a winter temperature of 50 degrees*. Oh, Mr. Free! Oh, Miss Jekyll! (who suffered from the same dreadful illusions). Why have you been deceiving us for so long? What is the secret of your strange grudge against the camellia? Ignorant persons like myself can be excused, but that you should spread this anti-camellia propaganda is unpardonable. For there is a good old English saying to the effect that 'A camellia is as hardy as a laurel', and it is true. If you wish to search for a feminine equivalent, you will not compare it to Mrs. Virginia Woolf nor Miss Rose Macaulay. You will compare it to Miss Dorothy Thompson or Miss

Elsa Maxwell, or any other of the female weight-lifters of international society.

But why compare it to anything, when it is incomparable?

§ v

The next day, I was down at the nurseries. (Did you know there were nurseries in London? Stretching for acres and acres, unsuspected, behind the most unpromising façades? No? Well, there are. But I won't tell you where they are, because I like to prowl about them alone. Muttering.)

Arrived at the nurseries, I demanded standard camellias. Within five minutes, I was reviewing a dozen of the same, walking up and down in front of them with a protruding lower lip, like General Goering in an off moment. I chose the tallest, the richest, the most exquisitely shaped. The price was enough to make you fall over backwards. But of all the investments I have ever made, this was the one there has been least cause to regret.

It arrived two days later. Meanwhile, we had been feverishly preparing its quarters, digging deep, draining, softening the soil, enriching it with leaf-mould and bone-meal. When it was transported across the lawn I had a sudden fear that it might be just too short, that it might not be visible from the other side.

The fear was groundless. The tree was exactly the right height. The result was perfect. I ran back to the terrace, to see it from the house. It looked as though it had been there from the beginning. Thirty . . . forty blossoms, glowing above the little wall, bringing round the Eye as it had never been brought before.

POSTSCRIPT.

Do you *wash* your camellia in your city garden? Or your lilacs, or your laurels, or whatever it may be? If not, you are a depraved and heartless person.

I wash mine, leaf by leaf. Standing on a chair, with a basin of soapy water balanced on the wall. Every inch of it is gently but thoroughly wiped over, and you would be amazed at the amount of dirt that comes off it, particularly from the stems.

It seems to me strange that you should wash your babies, and not your shrubs. Your shrubs, surely, are more in need of it? *They* have to stay out all day and all night, an ordeal to which your babies (unless you carry hygienic principles to excess) are seldom subjected.

Also, washing a tree or a shrub makes it more beautiful, brings out all sorts of hidden colours and unexpected tints. You cannot say that about washing a baby. It just goes on being a monotonous pink.

However . . . perhaps as a bachelor I am prejudiced.

CHAPTER VIII

ROSE AND CAVALIER

THE patient reader will long ago have realized that the chronology of this book has got completely out of hand. It isn't like a novel, in which girl accepts boy in December, at the time of Christmas roses, marries him in February with snowdrops in her hair, tells him a Great Secret just as the lilac is coming out, and . . . if the conventions have been observed and the weather is seasonable . . . presents him with a son and heir in the same week that the border chrysanthemums are coming into bloom.

It is much more like a ramble round a garden — a garden in which there is history in the fold of every leaf and memory, deep and colourful, in the heart of every flower.

Simply for my own satisfaction, I want to make a summary of our progress to date. There is another long pause immediately ahead of us, and I really must tidy up before we enjoy it together. So let us jot down the sequence of events up to the present, in the order of their occurrence.

October	We move in. Period of hatred.
November	Removal of poplar trees. Hatred continues.

February	Triangle drained and turfed. Small terrace built. Hatred not lessened.
Early March	Rhododendrons planted in apex. A few trees scattered about. A border of Siberian wallflowers by the fence. Boredom.
Late April	Wild hatred. Trees and flowers have only made triangle worse.
May and June	Rage and despair. Geometrical obsession. Triumph of triangle.
July	Inspiration. First reverse of triangle. Excitement.
August	Walls built round sides. Curved walls in centre. Nothing at apex, but excitement grows.
September	Curved path created. Main small beds and chief herbaceous border fixed. Still nothing at apex, but greenhouse with domed roof decided upon. Excitement mounts to fever pitch.

There, that's better. As though one had tidied up a room after a rather rowdy party. (By tidying up, I mean banging the cushions into shape, opening the windows, carrying seven empty gin bottles into the kitchen, and trying to arrange them to look as if they were only four, in order that Gaskin may not make any pointed remarks about the wine-merchant's bill in the morning.)

So here we are, with our walls built, and our beds in

order, waiting for the dome to go up, and the battle to begin. We do know, therefore, where we stand. But before we can advance, we must make sure of our allies. We look round. We see them, black, sleek and shining, stretched out in attitudes of abandonment in front of the fire.

Of course they have really been with us all the time, but we have been too busy to notice them. Or perhaps it would be truer to say that they have been too busy to notice *us*. There have been so many other urgent matters to demand their attention, causing them to dart in and out of the shrubbery, to make frenzied rushes up the drive, to stand with arched backs, regarding the traffic of the great world — one butcher's boy slowly trundling his bicycle up the hill — and then, overcome by the drama of this prospect, to career back again to the shelter of the front door, leaping like black demons through the hall, through the sitting-room, out into the comparative tranquillity of the terrace.

But now that they have made up their minds about London, and have been graciously pleased to accept it (with certain reservations) we must give them the attention that is their due. Even if we had no desire to do so, we could hardly avoid it. For we have reached the stage where the garden is crowding out all our other interests, where it has definitely supplanted the house as the main theatre of our existence. And as every cat has an exquisite instinct for the moment when it must take the centre of the stage, so these black shadows are to be found, more and more frequently, by our side, carrying out their feline duties of overseeing . . . patting bulbs, sitting firmly on a basket full of roots, and lying down on the exact spot which we have chosen for the next plant.

This is obviously a problem which will deeply concern us in the future, how far our love for the garden is going to compel us to curtail the divine right of cats. But for the moment, it is not to the future that we must look, but to the past. We must make another journey back to the country, and to Allways.

One hot day in July — it must be nearly seven years ago — I came up from Allways to hear *Rosenkavalier* at Covent Garden. I was alone during the performance, and alone when I came out, for opera has always been to me one of those things in life which are best appreciated in solitude. It would be wonderful to hear *Tristan* from a distance, in a great forest, with no one near; to lie on the pine-needles and see, through a gap in the trees, vague figures moving, and the rhythmic sweep of the conductor's arm.

To-night of all nights it was good to be alone, for it had been a superb performance. The music had sparkled like the waters of many fountains. It had danced and glittered; one felt that one could *see* it, that the delicate chords had drifted like silver phantoms across the stage. The singers were voices only, and their bodies mere illusions.

So I stepped out on to the pavement, prepared to wander through the fragrant alleys of the market, gloating over those remembered cadences, and sniffing, meanwhile, the intoxicating scent of crated melons and peaches, mingling with the earthy tang of vegetables.

'Oh, my dear, you're *just* the person I was looking for!'

I turned. I saw a lady who glittered from top to bottom. Who was she?

I made guttural noises at her.

'I know your cottage is full of mice, isn't it? Don't *tell* me!'

Cottage? Mice? What was it all about? Who was this person?

'And so,' she continued, 'as Laura said she couldn't *sleep* because of the mice' — (who was Laura?) — 'and Alan said you'd be gnawed *away*' — (who was Alan?) — 'I've decided to give you a present. Two heavenly kittens. Half Siamese.'

'Only half?' I asked sharply. Some remote Jewish great-great-grandmother must have started in her grave at that moment.

'Well, you see, there was a mistake. Laura is usually *most* careful about her animals. Almost cruel in a way, considering that after all we're all human, even cats, if you know what I mean. But apparently there was some mistake, and . . .'

'And I'm to take the blame?'

The lady laughed, glittering, like an agitated jelly, on the steps.

'Yes, darling. But honestly, they're divine. They've got all the Siamese things without any of the dis-advantages.'

'How do you mean?'

'Well, they've got that delicious wail. Like a very depressed sea-gull. They wail and wail and drive one *mad*. Which is something, you must admit.'

'Yes, I admit that.'

'Then they're chic beyond expression. Jet black. Very slim. Heart-breakingly elegant.'

'Go on.'

'I can't go on much more. But don't you think they sound divine?'

I thought for a moment. In a way, I agreed. That wail . . . that strange cry of the Siamese cat, which is so tragic and yet so silly, so bitter and yet so sweet! It echoed through my head, blending with the still trembling cadences of the music of the opera.

'All right,' I said. 'I'll have them.'

'Well, darling, you needn't be so *brusque*. Lots of people would adore them. After all, they're a phenomenon.'

'You said a mistake, before.'

'A happy error.'

We made arrangements about their delivery. (I still had no idea who she was.) As we parted, I said:

'They're boys, of course?'

'Of course.'

'Then I shall call them Rose and Cavalier.'

'But, darling, they're *both* boys.'

'Then it will be the first time that any boy has been called Rose.'

'It'll cast a shadow over his life.'

'If he's as elegant as you say, he'll be able to get over it.'

We made hurried notes about stations and times of delivery, on bits of envelopes. I left the anonymous jelly, who oozed into a shiny black Rolls. I remember wondering if Rose (or Cavalier) would look as sleek and elegant as the Rolls. Then I ceased to wonder, for the music seemed to start again. I walked into the darkness of the market, playing over the scenes in my head, living once again the enchanted moments of that exquisitely artificial masterpiece. But always, cats seemed to be dancing across the stage.

§ 11

A week later I was staying at the cottage with a man called George, when I received a telegram, which bore the mystic message:

ROES AND CAVIAR ARRIVE TWO THIRTY ALLWAYS
STATION STEPHANIE

'Somebody seems to be sending us a present,' I observed. 'But why roes?'

'Perhaps they're some peculiar sort of Russian fish. Is Stephanie Russian?'

'I haven't the vaguest idea what she is.'

'It's rather important. Some women think that anything that's black and smells like anchovy paste must
be caviar.'

'They only think that if they're paying for it themselves.'

'Shall we *not* fetch it?'

'I think we'd better. It's very hot, and it might go bad
and make terrible smells and start an epidemic.'

So we met the two-thirty.

The sleepy little station of Allways lies about six miles
from the village, and why it is called Allways I cannot
imagine, because at least six other villages lie nearer to
it. Indeed, it is difficult to understand why there is a
station in this part of the country at all. Hardly any
trains stop at it. They thunder through contemptuously,
on their way to the north, making the toy platform
quake and causing a momentary cyclone which whirls
fragments of newspaper high into the air, so that the
solitary porter clutches his cap and looks round in surprise, as though he had been hit below the belt.

But sometimes trains do stop, to discharge a load of
school-children, a farmer or two and a nice fat old
woman laden with parcels. These trains are charming,
tiny things, that puff their way so slowly across the fen
country that you can see them coming for ages. You feel
that you could go for a long walk and come back again
and the train would still be coming.

At last it arrived. One old woman and two school-children got out. The porter opened the door of the van, and deposited a large basket on the platform.

'That must be it,' said George. 'It's far too large for caviar. I knew it wouldn't be.'

'Well, it's not too large for roes.' And as I said that word I suddenly remembered. Roes . . . roes? Rose! And Cavalier!

'Cavalier!' I shouted, tugging George by the arm. 'Not caviar! Rose . . . not roes!'

'Roes, not roes? Are you mad?'

But we had by now reached the basket. And from inside came a faint and very plaintive wail — the seagull wail of the Siamese kitten. For the first time in my life, Cavalier was speaking to me.

All other thoughts were now banished, all disappointments. And all appointments too, if you will forgive the pun. For when new kittens are arriving at the house, it is as though royalty were expected. Everything must be swept aside for their comfort. Voices must be hushed, chairs arranged in convenient positions, special dishes prepared.

If you think this is too much trouble, then you will never know one of the greatest delights of all those to whom animals are, in a sense, more wonderful than men. You will never be admitted to one of the most distin-guished orders of mankind — the Companionship of the Cat.

§ III

We opened the door of the garden room. We put the basket softly in the middle of the floor.

Gently, in case it should frighten them, we cut the string that held the basket together.

Gently, with many creakings, we lifted back the lid. And there, blinking in the sunlight, were two of the strangest little bundles of fur that you have ever seen.

They were very thin, with huge eyes in which the blue of babyhood was already misted with the green of adolescence. They were jet black. Not a white hair was to be observed on their chests or on their paws. Their fur was sleek as newly-brushed sealskin. They were trembling a little.

They stayed quite still, their eyes slowly rotating round the room. As the eyes moved, you could see the black pupils narrow in the sunlight. You could see all sorts of things reflected in those eyes . . . the squares of the window-panes, the blue of the chintz, your own face, like an image in a convex mirror.

Neither of us moved. We stood like statues, watching the kittens. The kittens remained seated, imperially, in their basket. Although they were trembling, they were masters of the situation. They were aristocrats, and they knew it. There was nothing craven in their demeanour. 'Our limbs may be afflicted with a nervous flutter', they seemed to say, 'but that is a matter which should be beneath the notice of gentlemen. We are not interested in our limbs. We are only interested in this new residence to which you have transported us, and we are at the moment deciding whether it is the sort of residence to which we can give our approval.'

Still we did not move. There was no sound. The kittens stayed there, trembling. And then . . .

Through the open window drifted a feather. It was an ordinary hen's feather, snow-white, that had floated from the farmyard, over the hedges, on the summer wind. It flew into the room, remained poised for a minute, and sank to the floor. The kittens' eyes were riveted upon it. The feather twitched. The kittens stared at the feather. It twitched again . . . drifted into a corner. And suddenly one of the kittens, with a movement of exquisite grace, leapt from the basket, precipitated itself upon the feather, patted it, threatened it, retreated from it, sprang upon it again, and then, firmly, sat on it, and yawned.

I turned to George, and said, 'It's all right. They approve of us.'

§ I V

Those who love cats, who realize that they are not merely animated mouse-traps but intensely sensitive creatures who demand not only understanding but tact, and above all, *politeness*, will agree that the first few days in which a cat comes to stay in the house are days of considerable anxiety.

'We must put butter on their paws,' said George. 'And then they will be sure to stay.'

So we went out to the kitchen, got a large slab of butter and a knife, and returned to the garden room, where the kittens were still investigating the feather.

Until that day I had always adhered to the Paw-Buttering School of Thought. It was one of those theories that one learns at one's mother's knee, and it was jumbled up in my brain with a lot of other homely maxims, such as . . .

Collies are 'treacherous'
The sun puts fires out
If the moon shines on your face when you are asleep you go mad
Feed a cold and starve a fever
A lady is known by her shoes and her gloves
Cut toe nails square and finger nails round

We all have our store of these simple fragments of worldly wisdom which our mothers taught us, and though experience may sometimes make us change our opinions (though not about the toe nails), they will always be invested with a strange authority. They are the infantile mysteries. And one of them is, *Putting butter on cats' paws makes them stay.*

But in this case, it did not work. We started with the larger kitten, which was sitting in a position which is easier to draw than to describe.

As soon as the kitten was stroked, to prepare it for the buttering operation, it rose with charming politeness, purred loudly, and began to 'weave'. The weaving is shown thus:

More stroking. We tried to put a sedative touch into the stroking, to induce repose, but the kitten took it in quite a different way, and decided that a game was being played. So it assumed the attitude indicated below.

'Now's our chance,' said George. And though it seemed very unfair, we were forced to lift him up. George held him, and I prepared the dab of butter.

Cavalier was now extending his paw, as though he expected it to be gently and reverently kissed. When, instead of a kiss, he received a large dab of butter, an expression of faint disgust came over his face. However, we hoped for the best.

We set him down, with extreme care, as though he might explode. 'Ssh!' whispered George. 'Don't speak.'

We watched. Cavalier regarded the butter, still with the same expression of disgust. Then with a sudden sharp flick, he sent it flying. It landed exactly in the middle of the only respectable cushion in the cottage.

'I think,' said George, 'that if we want them to stay, we shall just have to rely on our own charm.'

We must have been very charming indeed. Far from showing any inclination to leave, they became our inseparable companions. They called us in the morning, scrambling up the wistaria and leaping straight through the open window on to the sheets, which they proceeded to decorate with an erratic pattern of paw-marks.

They quickly became keen gardeners ... they put their paws in every can of water, rolled on all the choicest seedlings, and darted out whenever they heard the wheelbarrow, in which they had a strange passion to ride. They even went for long walks with us, leaping with swift and graceful curves through the long grass, and then suddenly going mad, and chasing each other back to the house.

By the time the autumn came, I was very much in love with them both.

§ v

It was on a dull November day that I first noticed that something was wrong with Rose. We had been playing one of our favourite games together, which consisted in turning Rose over on his back, taking hold of his two front paws, and dragging him round the room. I should not at all encourage my friends to do this to me, but Rose seemed to love it, and when, purple in the face and panting, one released his paws and straightened oneself, he remained on his back, staring at one with astonishment, one paw flopping languidly in front of him. 'Did I tell you to stop? Did I intimate that I had had enough?'

But as he stayed there, lying back, in the light of the flickering fire, I saw a swelling. I felt his fur, and he mewed, as though in pain. One of the many traits in my character which I dislike is an incapacity to be 'cruel in order to be kind'. I ought to have dragged him under the light and dug about in his fur and disregarded his mews. But I was weak. I just lifted him up and stroked him and hoped that the swelling would go down.

But it didn't. It was worse in the morning. And since Rose meant a lot to me, by then, and since there were certain trees that I could never see without visualizing, in imagination, his black silhouette darting through the branches, and since there were hollows in the wood where always, it seemed, his ghost would be lurking . . . a taut, black ghost, poised to spring . . . I thought that the best thing to do would be to take him up to London at once, to see the best vet that money could buy. Which I did.

The vet was reassuring. He said that it was nothing to worry about, that the swelling would go away in time. However, in order to make sure, he said that he would keep Rose for a day or two.

He kept him. Those days were as miserable for me as for Rose. I thought of him in his cage, with nobody to understand him, nobody who knew that he liked being scratched on the left side of his face but not on the right, nobody who knew that he liked having his plate turned round for him when he was eating, because he was such an aristocratic cat that he could not be bothered to walk round to the farther side in order to finish his meal.

However, it was only for three days. When I went to fetch Rose again, his delight at seeing me made up for all that had gone by.

But it was short-lived delight. No sooner had I taken him out of his basket than I realized that he was ill, far worse than he had been when he went away. His nose was hot. His fur was dull. He refused all food. He could not even sit up. He sank down by the fire, and began to cough.

Rose had been put in a cage that had been previously occupied by a cat with the deadly feline influenza. He had caught it. The swelling had been nothing. If I had kept him at home he would have got over it. As it was, he caught this disease, in the fashionable, expensive establishment of the vet. And he was condemned to death.

No purr, when you stroked him. If you lifted him, only a sigh. None of those adorable movements . . . the arched back, the slow weaving round one's legs, the long, gracious stretch, the upturned face. Only a sad, hopeless sinking to the floor, and that ghastly cough.

I left him there, in the chair, late at night. I thought of him as a little kitten in the sunlight, with the feather drifting in through the window. I remembered his wild rushes through the long grass, his sweet warm elegance as he lay stretched on my bed, his climbs over the roof, his plaintive mews as he clamoured to be let in on a wintry night. And now . . . he had almost gone. He was just a cat, with eyes that were fast closing, and only a cough to remind him of what the world had once been, the world in which he had taken so much joy.

He died that night. We found him there, very still, in the early morning, by a fire whose ashes were still glowing. And Cavalier was prowling outside the room like a thing possessed, lifting up his voice in a bitter wail of protest against the scheme of life.

Well, we get over things. It may be sentimental to speak of the death of an animal as sadly as one would speak of the death of a human being. But when my dog had died, a year before, happily, naturally, in his sleep, I wondered how many of my friends could have given me this feeling of emptiness and loss.

And now, it was the same.

They say that if you have a crash when you are flying you must immediately get into another aeroplane, and take to the skies again within the hour, or you will lose nerve. It was on this principle that I tracked down the mysterious lady of the opera, discovered Rose's pedigree and birthplace, and invested in Rose II before a month had passed. He was a half-brother of Rose I, and an exact replica of him. Needless to say, Cavalier, sunk in mourning, would have none of him when he arrived.

He sat in a corner, his eyes blazing with grief and hatred, repelling all the advances which this thin, lonely little intruder made towards him. But gradually he relented. Maybe he saw in Rose II something of the beloved companion he had lost. Maybe his strange cat mind sensed that this was indeed his reincarnation. Whatever the reason, the growls grew fainter, the eyes blazed less fiercely. One day, miracle of miracles, there was a sniff, nose to nose. It was followed by a sharp cuff over the ear, but that was the first and last time that Cavalier attacked him.

When at last they came to London, they were not only inseparable — they were so exactly alike that you could hardly tell them apart.

We must get back to the garden, and I apologize for having held up the story. But Rose and Cavalier will be so constantly with us, leaping along the walls like animated Egyptian frescoes, helping us in the bedding out, the sowing and the watering, that you had to know something of their history. Also, they play a part in the battle that is about to begin — the Battle of the Dome.

CHAPTER IX

THE BATTLE OF THE DOME

THE first skirmishes in the great Battle of the Dome were so formal and so polite that they could hardly be regarded as more than a minor and very suburban 'incident'.

The Howards at Number 4 — my ideal neighbours — were at first a little alarmed when they heard what was afoot (though 'afoot' is hardly the right word for it). Indeed, in order to avoid the formation of any cloud that might mar our happy relationship, we both thought it advisable to have a cup of tea at our solicitor's. There, a pleasant compromise was effected. A plan was contrived by which the dome could be lowered nearly a foot and a half without spoiling the symmetry of the design. I also let Mr. Howard into a secret idea I had formed of covering the base with flowers, which he said would be swell.

We parted the best of friends, and expressed the wish that international problems might be settled as swiftly and agreeably. And I believe that to-day the Howards, who are persons of delicate taste, would quite miss the dome if any mishap should remove it from this world.

The inhabitants of Number 3 caused as little trouble as the inhabitants of Number 4. As for the lady at

Number 2, she wrote me a charming letter saying that she was quite sure that anything I put up would be delightful, and hoped that she would have the pleasure of gazing upon it as soon as possible.

There remained Mrs. H. at Number 1.

Normally I would have called upon Mrs. H., and after explaining what I wished to do, would have asked her if she had any objections. But it was impossible to do anything 'normally' where Mrs. H. was concerned. So I just let things slide.

The work proceeded apace. The big steel window frame for the south side arrived, and was cemented into the wall. I feared it might alarm the lady in the House-Next-Door, standing there all naked on the wall, with nothing happening above it. But on the only occasion that I saw her, flitting in her shadowy way across the lawn, she did not even pause to look at it.

The floor was covered with concrete, the boring business of drainage was achieved, the curved doors and windows for the front were put into position.

Breathlessly, we attended the dome.

Then, one day, it arrived. That is to say, they arrived. And it *did* look like Britain's Heroic Effort in Rearmament. It would not have surprised me to see Mr. Hore-Belisha dart out from behind a laurel bush, point to one of the immense steel girders, and proclaim, '*That* ought to teach the dictators'.

For really . . . well, you know how enormous that sort of thing looks, before it has been put up. I mean, things

135

like chimneys, and the town-hall clock, and statues of the Duke of Wellington. Too enormous.

I said to Gaskin, 'It can't be right. They must have made a mistake. It's an air-raid shelter after all.'

No, he said, dodging four men who were staggering under the weight of an even larger girder than usual. This was the dome, all right.

Even as he said it, Mrs. H.'s car drove up to the entrance of the drive. I retreated into the shadow of the back door.

Mrs. H. emerged, slammed the door of her car, and began to walk down the drive. Then, as though she had had an electric shock, she stopped dead. Her eyes fixed themselves on the great girders, the steel bars, the carefully piled, crescent-shaped pieces of heavy glass. Her nostrils . . . I swear it . . . her nostrils dilated.

I don't know how long Mrs. H. stayed there. It seemed an age. But when at last she pulled herself together, and stumped towards her own front door, there was a look of grim resolution about the set of her mouth that boded ill for someone, and that someone was me.

For at least five minutes, I wished that the whole thing was at the bottom of the sea. I wished that instead of going in for domes and flowers I had gone in for cellars and mushrooms. The latter would obviously have been more patriotic. During air-raids, one would

have been able to sit in the cellar, and offer the mushrooms, like a perfect gentleman, to trembling women
and children. 'Champignons à la Chlorine', one would
have said, keeping the party bright.

I went in, and kicked up some warmth from a dying
fire. Why, oh why, did Mrs. H. always make me think of
war?

§ 11

War, however, it was to be. And the first assault was
delivered on the following morning at the grey hour of
10 a.m.

For the moment, Mrs. H. was forgotten. Even the
dome was not in my thoughts. I was sitting by the fire,
holding a pad in my hand on which were written the
words, 'Blank. A New Novel by Beverley Nichols.
Chapter 1'. When one is in that condition, one forgets
the outside world of domes, towers and temples. One
even forgets the existence of people like Mrs. H.

Into this scene of lofty abstraction, burst Gaskin,
strictly against orders. Mrs. Heckmondwyke, he said
in tones of urgency, was coming down the drive. Should
she be admitted? The front door-bell rang. Of all
moments in life I most dislike those moments when the
front door-bell rings. Is one in? Is one out? Is one done
up? Has one shaved? Is there anything incriminating
on the sofa? And who the hell *is* it, anyway?

But when it was Mrs. H. at the other end of the bell, the agony was intensified. The power of thought seemed to desert me. 'What do you think?' I demanded. 'I suppose I ought to be. No, I won't. Wait a minute. I don't know. Let me think.'

'You'll have to see her *some* time,' Gaskin reminded me.

The door-bell rang again.

'It's absolute persecution.'

'She's sure to know you're in.'

I realized that Gaskin was right. So I flew upstairs, in order . . . well, in order to come down again. In order to make an entrance, in fact. No sooner had I done so than I remembered, with a shock, that I had left the sketch of the dome lying in full view on the piano. Mrs. H. would be bound to see it. There would be no chance of denying anything now. But then, how could one have denied anything, with the drive full of Britain's Heroic Effort in Rearmament?

At the drawing-room door, I coughed before entering. Mrs. H.'s nose was certain to be glued to the sketch of the dome. And sure enough, when I entered, she was moving rapidly away from the piano, and the sketch was in a different position.

We greeted each other warmly. Wouldn't she sit down? Yes, very cold indeed, wasn't it. No, really, nothing much in my garden either. Pause.

'But then, of course, you *can't* expect to have anything very much, can you, with so many men tramping about the place?' said Mrs. H. 'How thankful you will be when they are all gone!' Meaning, of course, how thankful she would be herself.

Another pause.

'And by the way,' she added, as though it were an after-thought, 'while we *are* on this subject, I wonder if you could give us some idea of when the drive will revert to normal?'

'Normal?'

'Normal,' she repeated, rather more loudly. 'Of course I don't mind it being almost impossible to drive the car through the gates. One's getting quite used to *that*.' A tender smile accompanied these words. 'Ever since . . .' She was about to say 'Ever since you came', but left the sentence unfinished. She went on. 'I was merely thinking about all the houses in the Close. Very well built, of course. But there is a limit to what any house will stand, don't you think?' She looked up to the ceiling and saw a small crack, which had been caused by a brief but violent bout of physical exercise in the bedroom upstairs. 'Ah, yes! I see you've got it too. Not so badly as at Number 1, though. All our ceilings are cracking.' She smiled, martyr-like. 'One's fond of one's little house.'

'I'm very sorry indeed,' I said. I really was. 'But the men should all have gone by to-morrow, and after that, I don't think there'll be any more.'

'No?' She smiled again. 'Well,' she sighed, 'we can but . . .'

Presumably she had intended to say, 'We can but

hope'. But the sentence froze on her lips. For at that moment Rose appeared in the doorway. Very demure he looked, with his head slightly on one side, as he advanced with measured steps towards us.

The reaction of Mrs. H. was immediate. She uttered a shrill cry, pushed back her chair, and crouched in a position of exaggerated terror.

'Please! *Please!* Don't let him come near me!'

I picked up Rose. He began to purr. His green eyes remained fixed on Mrs. H. His expression was one of curiosity, not unmingled with contempt.

'Oh, thank you,' she breathed. 'There's . . . there's no chance that he will escape?'

'None at all,' I said.

Although I love cats, I have every sympathy with those persons afflicted by the morbid disease of ailurophobia. Have we not the authority of Shylock to remind us

> Some men there are love not a gaping pig,
> Some that are mad if they behold a cat?

Men as varied as Ronsard, Alphonse Daudet, and — ironically enough — the late Lord Roberts, were all filled with horror at the proximity of cats, whose presence in a room they claimed to be able to detect even before they had seen it.

But Mrs. H. was not a true ailurophobe. With my own eyes I had seen Rose, on more than one occasion, weaving round her ankles in the drive. And though, being an ill-bred woman, she had eventually waved him away, she had done so with no evidence of haste, let alone of fear. It was obvious that this little scene was being put on for my benefit.

'Might we . . .' she began, faintly. 'Could we . . . perhaps you would allow me to open the window?'

'I'll put Rose in the kitchen,' I said.

When I returned, Mrs. H. was standing by the open window, fanning herself. She looked exceedingly healthy.

'So foolish of me,' she sighed. 'Just something that comes over me. I can tell when they're in the room.' She attempted a shudder, without great success. 'Lord Kitchener was the same.'

'Lord Roberts,' I corrected.

'Kitchener, I think,' she repeated, sweetly. And then — 'I must be going.'

I looked at her with surprise. Was it possible that she was about to leave without making any reference to the dome? I felt a curious sense of relief, and yet of disappointment — the sort of feeling one has when the dentist says that he doesn't think he'll take it out to-day, but that we'd better wait till next week.

Then she paused. Casually, very casually, her eye wandered to the design that was lying on the piano. I held my breath. Now it was coming.

'Sketching?' she inquired brightly.

For reply, I blew my nose.

She went over to the piano, and held the sketch up to

the light. 'Charming,' she said, 'Quite charming. What is it?'

'It's a design for a greenhouse.'

'A greenhouse?' She raised her eyebrows and made a little clucking noise with her tongue against her teeth. 'Well, well,' she said. 'I suppose there are places where it wouldn't be out of place. Hampton Court, perhaps. Yes. At the end of one of those long avenues in Hampton Court, it would be delightful.' She laid the sketch down, and began to walk towards the door. Then once again she paused. In the most amiable tones she said, 'Oh, yes! That reminds me. Such a silly thing, you must forgive me for mentioning it . . . but I heard some absurd rumour about a dome for the little greenhouse you're putting up here. I knew, of course, that there couldn't be anything in it, because . . .'

'But I'm afraid . . .' I began.

'Because,' she interrupted, 'of course it would be quite out of the question. Naturally. Ancient lights.'

'I've been into the matter of ancient . . .'

'Ancient lights,' snapped Mrs. H. again, with that awful smile still firmly fixed on her face. 'You know all about *them*, of course. Very tricky.' (She made it sound as if ancient lights were some tribe of elderly witches, under her personal direction.) 'Very tricky indeed. But, of course, you know that. I remember reading somewhere that you had been trained for the Bar, but had to give it up. Terrible, it must have been for you, to have to go in for writing.'

'But I'm afraid,' I said, loudly, and a little breath-lessly, 'the question of ancient lights does not apply in this case.'

'Oh, but *yes*! Quite. It does. Everywhere. Ancient lights.' She jerked the words out as if somebody were standing behind her and squeezing her ribs.

She turned again to the door. 'So glad we've had this little talk,' she said. 'So much better to save mis-understanding. And money. Naturally you wouldn't wish to proceed with any work that had to be pulled down as soon as it was put up.'

'But Mrs. Heckmondwyke,' I said, trying to remain calm, 'nobody else in the Close has the least objection.'

'Ah! So the others have been consulted, have they?'

'I have mentioned the subject, yes.'

'But not to me. May I ask why?'

I shrugged my shoulders. The only answer I could have given would have sounded extremely discourteous.

'Perhaps I'm not supposed to have any taste? Or perhaps there's an idea that because I wear spectacles, I'm almost completely blind? Yes? It would be interest-ing to know.'

'But really,' I ventured, 'we all know that you have perfect taste. That's why I can't imagine how you could object to . . .'

'The sudden appearance of the Crystal Palace at the bottom of my garden? Yes?'

'A very small domed greenhouse, in the Regency manner, of which you will only see a small portion of the roof in winter, and nothing at all in summer.' I went to the piano and took up the sketch.

'Not ...' she exclaimed (as though a determined assault were being made upon her virtue) ... 'not that!'

'But please *look* at it!'

She stood there, holding the design in her fat, smartly gloved fingers. It fluttered a great deal, because she was shaking with rage. I awaited the explosion. It came in a most unexpected manner. She suddenly burst into peals of hysterical laughter.

'Oh dear! Oh dear! Forgive me!' She was quite overcome. She wiped her eyes. 'I had no idea. This! And to think that I suggested Hampton Court!'

'Very amusing,' I muttered.

She threw the design away. The laughter ceased as quickly as it had begun.

'Well,' she snapped, 'I'm delighted to have seen it. More than delighted. Because now I know that there can be absolutely no question of its going up. I shall issue a writ.'

'But Mrs. H.', I cried, in a last effort to make her see reason, 'I've already spent a great deal of money on it. The whole thing has been specially designed and made. It's going up to-morrow.'

'Then it will come down the day after.'

'It will do nothing of the sort. All the other residents of the Close have agreed to it.'

'I care nothing for the other residents.'

'And it would be impossible for you to prove in a court of law that you were being in the least ... incommoded.'

'Incommoded?' she exclaimed. 'Well, of course, other people may have different ideas as to the meaning of the word "incommode". Not being a writer, of course, I can't be expected to know. I should have *thought* — of course I may be wrong — that *some* people ... not writers, but just ordinary common people like me ... *some* people might be slightly incommoded if they found that their garden was to be permanently plunged into pitch darkness.'

'But, Mrs. Heckmon ...' ·

'*Slightly* incommoded,' she repeated, her voice becoming more shrill. 'I should have thought that some people ... not geniuses, but drab, suburban people like me ... would have expressed just a hint of incommodation' — (she paused and gulped) — 'if they had bought a house in Heathstead only to find themselves living in the shadow of a Mahometan Exhibition.'

I was so worked up, by now, that my face twitched into an uncontrollable grin at these words.

It was too much for Mrs. H. She seized her bag and marched to the door without saying another word. She was through it before I could open it for her. And through the front door too, opening it and slamming it before Gaskin could get near it. I went back to the sitting-room in a daze, feeling as though a cyclone had passed over me.

At that precise moment, I heard the final lorry clatter slowly down the drive, stopping with a bang outside. Exactly as it did so, a small piece of plaster fell from the ceiling. I wished that it had been much bigger, and that Mrs. H. had been standing underneath it.

CHAPTER X

ONE THING LEADS TO ANOTHER

THREE weeks later I went down to the greenhouse with a letter in my hand. It was a very important letter, and it had to be read, for the twentieth time, in appropriate surroundings.

The light was beginning to fade, and a few specks of rain were falling.

As I opened the door, the crisp clean tang of chrysanthemums welcomed me. The chrysanthemums were really an unwarranted extravagance, because I was not yet 'going in' for chrysanthemums, and there were enough here to stock the whole house, after one year's division. There were flowers with chocolate-coloured petals, backed with saffron. Every petal was as exquisitely curled as if some very meticulous coiffeur, with green fingers and golden tongs, had sat up all night over each adorable head. There were *boules de neige* that really *were* like snowballs, and set your mind asking a lot of pleasantly unprofitable questions as to whether these were the whitest of all white flowers, or whether the white of the madonna lily or the white of the gardenia was even more immaculate. (I think the chrysanthemum has it, don't you?) There were two 'cascade' chrysanthemums, poised over the shelves like frozen spray, and a mass of yellows and bronzes. And always there was that enchanting odour, one of the few masculine perfumes of nature.

Did you ever make a list of perfumes according to gender? The smell of new-mown hay is male, the scent of a wild rose is female. The smoke from a bonfire is a male scent, and so is the scent of spray, and heather, and of the leaves of the laurel. The list of scents that are feminine is so much longer and more extensive that women must allow us these small privileges.

But here we are, talking about the gender of scents, when there is one scent so overpoweringly feminine that we are in duty bound to follow it — the scent that hovers, like a danger signal, over the tracks of Mrs. H.

Well, I am going to do something which is against all the rules of story-telling. I am *not* going to follow it. I am writing this book for fun, and I am fed up with Mrs. H.

And it would seem that she also was fed up with me, judging from the letter I was holding. Its complexity forbids quotation from it. It was full of references to 'learned counsel', and liberally sprinkled with quotations from the case of *Smoggett* v. *Bloggs* (or some such persons who had had dome trouble in the reign of Queen Anne); but through the mist of legal jargon I could see, faintly waving, a flag of truce.

And very glad I was to salute that flag, for there had been times when I had been really alarmed. The worst moment was perhaps when Mrs. H., with a cunning born of desperation, had suddenly arrived at the front door with twelve — yes, *twelve* — very assorted males and females, who, on account of their number, I took to be the jury. A moment's reflection would have revealed to me the foolishness of such a supposition. Apart from the fact that the case never came into court, and that therefore no jury was ever called, it should have been evident to a child of six that even Mrs. H. could not kidnap an entire jury and march it round my garden at her command. But when you are involved in a lawsuit, you lose all sense of proportion. The butcher, the baker, and the candlestick maker no longer appear to you as tradesmen, they become potential allies or enemies.

'Just a few witnesses,' Mrs. H. had hissed to Gaskin, as she led this astonishing procession on to the terrace. I watched, in agony, from an upstairs window. And when they had gone, both Gaskin and I were plunged into depression. Even the reassurances of my own lawyer, coupled with his suggestion that Mrs. H. should be sued for trespass, were inadequate to cheer me up.

That was the day that I went out and bought the chrysanthemums. It was what might be called a 'gesture'. If the dome had to come down, at least I could comfort myself with the thought that for a few nights it had sheltered a host of lovely flowers. Apart from that, I had an instinct that perhaps if the flowers were once installed, they would be there for always. Besides, two could play at juries. If Mrs. H. could get hold of twelve people on her side, I could get hold of twelve people on mine. And when I had got hold of them, I should take them down to the dome, throw wide the door, show them the flowers in all their beauty, and cry, 'This, gentlemen, is the outrage at which you are asked to assist! To throw these frail blossoms out into the cold! To send them to a swift and certain death! Is it possible that any British man, that any British woman, worthy of the name, could etc. etc.?'

Well, all that was over now. And the flowers would be allowed to sleep in peace.

§ 11

Well, here we are in the greenhouse, at the end of October, looking up through the roof of semi-opaque glass. You have no idea how fascinating it is to gaze through such a roof. It is like being in a diving bell. The birds that skim overhead pass like the shadows of fishes, the branches of the trees might be waving sea-weed, and the light is dim and aqueous . . . though I hasten to assure you that there is a constant stream of golden sunlight from the main south window, and a plentiful infiltration from the glass-panelled doors.

Of course, it has all sorts of disadvantages. Too much light on one side, too little on the other. Even as I stand there, I realize that from now onwards a large part of my life will be spent turning pots round, away from the light, so that the plants that are in them may have a

chance of straightening themselves. But what pleasanter occupation could life hold, when you come to think of it? There is no more agreeable way of spending a lazy hour than by going down to the greenhouse and gravely swivelling all the pots whose plants are craning eagerly to the light. It makes one feel very grand and powerful. Schoolmasters, I suspect, must constantly enjoy this sensation. 'Do not look out of the window, Jones,' they say, 'or I shall turn you over.' 'Do not look out of the window, schizanthus,' I echo, 'or I shall turn you round.'

However, we cannot go on lingering like this in the greenhouse. Great adventures await us. I would bet you cannot possibly guess what those adventures are. They're connected with the greenhouse, it is true, but they are the last things that you would expect.

They were the last things that I expected myself. But that is the way of life. The greatest discoveries are always made by men who are looking for something else. From Columbus down, the most celebrated explorers have been tripping over things by accident, rather than locating them by design. They set out to climb an obscure mountain, and fall over an equally obscure cliff. It does not seem to make very much difference. Doctors do not like you to remind them of it, but a vast amount of medical knowledge is the result of pure chance. A fever is engendered in some wretched rabbit with the object of throwing new light on the influenza germ. Nothing is discovered about the influenza germ, but a pretty little theory is born about the early stages of malaria. Men strike oil when they are looking for diamonds, and run into gold when they are digging a potato patch. It is all summed up in a little poem which I have always thought was the only really perfect example of the triolet, the thistledown of poetry:

> I intended an Ode,
>   And it turn'd to a Sonnet.
> It began *à la mode*,
> I intended an Ode;
> But Rose cross'd the road
>   In her latest new bonnet;
> I intended an Ode;
>   And it turn'd to a Sonnet.

And so it was with me. I intended a Toolshed. And it turned to a Fernery.

Let me be more explicit. Now that I had the greenhouse, I was determined that in certain things it should be self-supporting. There was so much of the city about it, with its electric light and its artificial heat, that I felt it was vital to redress the balance in favour of nature. That was the reason why I had insisted on a tank of fresh rainwater, instead of having water laid on. It was also the reason why, at this moment, I made a decision which seemed trivial at the time, but was to lead to a hundred unexpected excitements.

I decided to make my own leaf-mould.

You would not think that such a small thing would alter a man's life, would you? Yet it altered mine.

Try to see it as I saw it, in that tempestuous month. We lived to the rhythm of falling leaves. Every leaf that flew over the wall seemed like a fragment of lost treasure, a spinning coin of fertility that eluded me. For there was nowhere ... no, not a single foot or inch of land, where this treasure could be stored. I *must* make leaf-mould. I *must* have a toolshed, where I could build a little cage, and keep the door open, and press down the moist fragrant stuff, and stir it up, and sniff it, and put it into sacks. But where, oh where? (How many thousands of city gardeners have asked themselves the same question!)

And all the time, the chorymbus of autumn was getting into my veins, making the problem more and more urgent. I wasn't thinking only of the greenhouse, I was thinking of all the other things that inflame the hearts of gardeners at this hurrying season. For the bulb catalogues were arriving, glittering with larger and yellower daffodils, grape hyacinths the size of bananas, and other novelties, which were guaranteed to 'burst into spikes of dazzling blue 'ere winter's snows have fled'. I sat down with a paper and pencil, as in the old days, and ran amok, as though I still had acres of land in which to give these darling things a home. And suddenly I realized that if all these bulbs were ordered, I should be obliged to plant them on Hampstead Heath. Which made me feel very mean and squalid, like something sitting on the steps of an institution, munching stale bread.

'But I am not on the steps of an institution,' I swore to myself. 'I am munching nothing. Not yet. It is too ridiculous. I am the owner . . . (at least, I shall be when I have paid off the bank) . . . of a delightful residence, with a most alluring little garden.' Aye, there was the rub. It really was almost too little to be funny, wasn't it?

I clenched my teeth. No, it was *not* too little. I refused to be browbeaten like this. Had not the garden already been transformed, by superhuman efforts, into something that seemed three times as large as it really was? Yes, it had! Then why shouldn't there be further transformations, which would make it seem four times larger . . . five times, six times?

I pushed aside the catalogues and drew back the blinds. Dusk was falling. There was a high wind, and the leaves were coming down fast. I thought of the delight that would be mine if I could gather all those leaves together, and bend closely over them, savouring their sweet essences, and thinking of the new life that they would bring, by their corporate death, to the wasted earth outside. And I determined that a place should be found for that leaf-mould, even if I had to sacrifice the bathroom, or build some monstrous erection on the chimney-tops.

§III

So once more, Making-the-Most-of-It was the order of the day.

I began by spending long hours in the box-room, sitting on a crate full of old blankets, sneezing. If you switched your electric torch round the plaster ceiling, you saw all sorts of places, where, at a pinch, a gable window might be built, and at another pinch, a sort of platform might be erected under the gable window, which could be turned into a depository for leaf-mould. Quite seriously, those ideas did occur to me. I even thought of knocking off the roof altogether, and creating some sort of extension to the garden up there, which only shows you to what heights of folly Making-the-Most-of-It will conduct a man. I was only deterred from these schemes by a timely reference to my lease, which contained all sorts of clauses about 'all that messuage'. And as I stepped gingerly over the rafters, it occurred to me that any very large amount of earth would certainly fall through the ceiling, and cause a hell of a messuage.

So the box-room was out.

The next place to demand attention was the little patch that lay in the shadow of the House-Next-Door. It was only the size of a kitchen table, but it was *space*, and it was mine, and it was doing nothing to justify itself. Owing to the fact that it was largely filled with privet, you could best gauge its proportions if you got on to a chair in the bedroom, and lay with your stomach on the window-ledge, so perhaps I had rather a hazy impression of it. At any rate, when Mr. Peregrine arrived and learned that I thought one might build a nice little something there and store leaf-mould on the roof . . . with perhaps a lead box too, from which festoons of exquisite ivy-geraniums would glow in the gloom, he shook his head, and said it would never do.

'We do not wish to *deter* you, sir,' he began, as usual. And then he proceeded to deter me good and proper. Such a roof as I contemplated could not be made suitable for leaf-mould. If anything heavy were put on it, collapse would ensue. If collapse did not ensue, it would leak, and poisonous juices would shower them-selves on to anybody who might be below. If it did not leak, it would go bad (i.e. anything that was on the roof would go bad). The leaf-mould would become a nest of shuddery insects. It would smell like nothing on earth. The roots of the flowers would rot. The local authorities would have fits. There was no end to the disasters that Mr. Peregrine foresaw, 'although we do *not* wish to deter you', he concluded.

So that was out, too.

What about a tunnel? If only there had been a cellar, something might have been created from that. Also, one could have grown mushrooms. But there was no cellar.

I thought of 'taking in' part of the drive. True, it was not mine; it was common to all of us. But if one were to go out in the dead of night, and scrape up an inch of concrete at a time, perhaps the others would not notice it? And if, in the meantime, one were particularly charming to everybody, and showered compliments about, and presented bottles of vintage port, perhaps people might be lulled into a sort of stupor of acquiescence?

I even thought of lying in wait for Mrs. H., and stealing out to switch off the lights of her car whenever she left it in the road. Then I could rush back, ring the bell, and tell her that her lights were off, and might I have the honour of turning them on for her? Such actions, surely, would create a body of goodwill sufficient to offset any momentary surprise or indignation that might be occasioned by my scraping up a few measly feet of drive.

However, when I began to measure things, and to study the lie of the land, it was clear that if the drive were more than a foot narrower it would be almost impossible to squeeze my own car out of it, even if it were smeared with vaseline and driven by a genius in a high wind. So *that* was out, too.

§ I V

We really are getting to the leaf-mould. And from the leaf-mould to the toolshed, and from the toolshed to the ferns. They are waiting round the corner, spreading their fans ready for our inspection, fans that are lined with gold and silver. (Did you know about the gold and silver ferns? No? Well, you just wait.)

And the way to get to them, strange as it may seem, is through a narrow passage in the garage.

It happened like this.

Owing to the aforesaid lack of space all the gardening tools had to be kept in the garage. At first there were so few that they were easily stowed away, but gradually the development of the garden called for an imposing collection of spades, rakes, hoes, trowels, forks, shears, and all the rest of it. Well, you know how it is with gardening tools. You have exactly the right place for them, but somehow they are never in it. You are in a hurry and you throw the rake on the floor instead of hanging it up, and there it stays, baring its teeth in a perpetual snarl.

Now it does not matter if it bares its teeth in a roomy old toolshed in the country, but if it does so in a small and what is known as 'bijou' garage, it matters very much indeed. Every night I would swirl through the front gates, skid round in an elegant circle, just avoid scraping the wings on the garage doors, jam on the brakes, and then . . . crash! the whole of Heathstead was awakened by the din of gardening tools clattering about the cement floor.

You would think that once you had made such an elementary mistake, you would not make it again. This is just where you would be wrong. You make it again *and* again, and one night, I made it once too often. I swept in. There was a loud report. I descended, to find the point of a new pair of shears firmly embedded in a front tyre.

This was too much of a good thing. Cursing loudly, I opened the door into the little passage which led to the garden, and threw the shears through it. Then I gathered all the tools in sight and shot them unceremoniously into the same place. And at that very moment the problem of the toolshed was solved. The *passage* was the toolshed! It was nearly seven feet long, and all it needed was another door, at the garden end, to keep the rain out.

Upon which pleasing reflection, I went to bed.

§ v

In a surprisingly short time the conversion of the passage was achieved. The new door was hung, the shelves were up, and boxes of leaf-mould, lime, sand and bone-meal were on the floor. The toolshed was complete. It seemed much larger than you would have thought possible. Two fat men and one thin woman could have stood in it, without anything particularly repulsive happening.

'You know,' I said to Joseph, one morning, 'there's still a lot of room left on these shelves. If only we had a bit more light, we could use this place for cuttings.'

Joseph glanced up at the roof (which was solid), looked at me, and grinned.

'No,' I replied sternly, 'we *can't* put in a glass roof. Mrs. H. would go mad.' I looked up too. 'Or could we?'

Needless to say, we did. Another week, and the glass roof was in. And it wasn't Mrs. H. who went mad. I went mad myself. For the glass roof seemed to make practically no difference to the light. The place was still plunged in perpetual gloom, and any cuttings which one might have put in it would have been condemned to an early death.

For several days I pottered about in this dark, draughty place, trying to think of ways by which the light could be increased. It was delightful to have all this room for tools, the leaf-mould and the other things, but the waste of the extra space was maddening.

If it had not been for a second accident, it would probably be maddening me to this day.

The accident occurred when Joseph dropped a large pane of glass in the drive. I hurried out to see what had happened and asked him to sweep it up as quickly as possible, to avoid any complaints from Mrs. H.

Too late! I might have known that this was one of the occasions when Mrs. H. simply had to be there. Hardly had Joseph hurried off, than she *was* there, standing by my side.

I removed my hat, and murmured the usual things. It was the first time that we had spoken since the Battle of the Dome and I was interested to see what attitude Mrs. H. had decided to adopt. I was soon to learn. It was one of martyrdom, of shrinking resignation. It did not become Mrs. H. at all.

'I'm so sorry to trouble you,' she murmured, 'but this glass?' (She did not look at me when she spoke, nor did she look at the glass. She looked heavenwards, and flinched, as though she were expecting a blow on the chin.)

'Joseph is sweeping it up immediately,' I replied. And here he was, emerging with a broom.

'So kind,' she breathed, still looking heavenwards. 'I only ask because I was just going to take the car out.'

I glanced to the top of the drive. To my dismay, a large lorry was trying to negotiate the corner. Mrs. H. also saw it. There had been so many lorries arriving for me that we both assumed that this must be one of mine too. 'To take the car out,' she repeated, in tones that were not quite so fragile as before. 'Always providing, of course, that the lorry will allow me. Have you any idea how long it will be?'

The lorry advanced a little farther, and stuck again. Oh joy! It was a coal lorry, and it was Mrs. H.'s coal-merchant.

'I really couldn't say, Mrs. Heckmondwyke. How long does your coal-merchant usually take to get round the corner?'

She gave a sickly smile, and shook her head. A quick retreat into trembling resignation was obviously the only answer to this question. But she could not tear herself away just yet. Her curiosity was too intense. She glanced towards the garage. 'Another little dome?' she inquired, with an heroic attempt at gaiety.

I replied in the negative.

'Not even a teeny-weeny one? May I make sure?'

Before I could stop her, she had tripped into the garage, opened the door, and was standing in the toolshed.

An expression of great concern appeared on her face.

'Oh, dear!' she cried, looking up to the glass roof. 'Do you think that is wise?'

'In what way?'

'To have a large piece of glass laid flat on to the roof? If anybody should step on it in the dark . . .'

'The only person who is likely to walk about on top of the garage roof after dark is a burglar,' I retorted, somewhat sharply. 'So from the point of view of the general safety of the Close, I should think it would be very wise indeed.'

Sweet smiles from both of us rounded off this remark.

'And what will you put on these dear little shelves?' inquired Mrs. H. 'Of course, nothing would *grow* on them, not in the dark like this.'

She glanced at me, waiting for a reply. None came. She had me here, and she knew it. It wasn't any use trying to bluff about gardening with Mrs. H. She was too good a gardener.

She decided to prolong the torture.

'Mushrooms might do,' she continued airily. 'Or

162

perhaps you were thinking of turning it into an aquarium and flooding the entire Close? Yes?'

I could still think of nothing to say. It was maddening. Here she was, gloating over the fact that a great deal of money had been expended in order to create a place that was entirely useless. And I was powerless to deny it.

'Watercress?' she suggested, as though speaking to herself. She shook her head. 'One or two aspidistras? Perhaps. Moss?' She paused.

Moss? Something suddenly registered, in the back of my mind.

'It's certainly damp enough for *moss*,' she repeated.

Oh, Mrs. H., what a pity you ever said that word 'Moss'! A pity for you — not for me. For your sarcastic words about shade and moss and damp woke an echo in my memory, an echo that carried me back, far back, to a certain waterfall on a Dartmoor river, where as a boy I had often scrambled up the granite rock in search of ferns. There may seem but a faint connection between the stuffy London toolshed and those green and airy spaces, but it was strong enough for me.

'Ferns!' I said, not thinking of Mrs. H. There had been a lovely cluster of ... what was it? What was the name? I used to remember. Just by a pool of water that was black in the shade and amber in the sunlight. *Asplenium* ... I racked my brains. *Asplenium fontanum*. That was it.

'What did you say?'

163

I must have spoken aloud. The voice of Mrs. H. called me back to reality.

'*Asplenium fontanum*,' I repeated. Even as I said it, a great decision was made. 'One of the commoner varieties of the ferns that I shall be growing in here.'

'Oh!' Mrs. H.'s face fell. She glanced around at the little shelves, at the roof, at the door, 'So this,' she said, 'is to be the fernery?'

And that is how it came about.

CHAPTER XI

RHAPSODY IN GREEN

It was now evident that through the fall of a pane of glass I had been propelled on to a path which would lead to a number of unforeseen adventures.

'Propelled' is perhaps too strong a word. Even without the assistance of Mrs. H. we should probably have come to ferns, sooner or later, for the simple reason that there was nothing else to come to. But I should not have concentrated on them with so fierce an attention. For to tell the truth — strictly between you and me and the toolshed — I thought ferns were rather a bore. I had only once visited the ferneries at Kew, and then I had come out again after a couple of minutes, deciding that it wasn't worth while to risk double pneumonia merely for the pleasure of gazing at a lot of green leaves, which looked very much alike. Naturally, I was familiar with the commoner adiantums and polypodiums, but I didn't get any great thrill out of them.

Nor, I would guess, do you. When there are so many lovely flowers in the world, why should you bother about leaves? When you can have all the colours of the rainbow, why should you confine yourself to green? When there are so many exquisite scents, why restrict yourself to something so faint, so monotonous as the scent of a fern?

Why, indeed? I should have agreed, if anybody had asked me these questions, two years ago. And it is because I now know how much I missed by such an attitude, that I want you to try to realize it too. Please forget all you ever knew about ferns, and believe me when I tell you that here is a new chapter in your gardening life, a chapter that will not be monotonous, nor dull, but full of colour, excitement, fragrance, and an endless complexity of design.

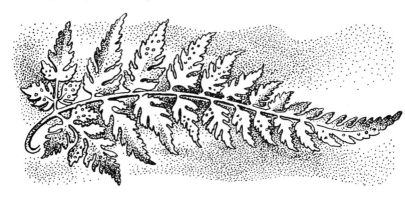

§ 11

We will start at the very beginning, under a sense of compulsion, rather than of inclination. We don't *mind* going in for ferns — (for that matter, we don't mind going in for any green thing except speckled laurels and monkey-puzzles) — but we certainly should not be doing it if it were not for Mrs. H. She is forcing our hands. We have announced to her that there is to be a fernery, and since we are quite certain that sooner or later she will have poked her way into it, we have got to do something about filling it with ferns.

Well, the first thing to do is to buy a book. I admit that this is the first thing that I did, and it was through this book that I got my first thrill, my first sense that here, perhaps, were excitements which had not been guessed. (You can hardly count the scrambling over the rocks as a boy. The thrill, on those occasions, was more concerned with the climb than with its object.)

The first book I bought was called *Choice Ferns for Amateurs*, and I opened it with a yawn. The yawn stopped on the second page. For here, at the end of a paragraph of very pedestrian prose, was this delicious sentence:

'The violet-scented *Nephrodium fragrans* is now abundant on the mountains of Japan.'

I rolled that sentence over on my tongue. It was full of music. *Nephrodium fragrans* was a phrase that might have fluted through an ode by Keats. A violet-scented fern was a conceit that suggested a lyric by Edgar Allan Poe. And the sudden connection of this fantastic, unlikely creation with the distant mountains of Japan brought the whole thing into the domain of Coleridge.

I made a mark against that sentence. Somehow or other I should get hold of a violet-scented fern, even if its roots had to be dipped in perfume. I was still thinking, you will observe, in terms of Mrs. H.

But Mrs. H. was quickly fading from my mind. For

the next paragraph to be pencil-marked was headed
'Gold and Silver Ferns'.

Here there were no magic sentences. The prose was of
the usual 'garden handbook' variety. I read:

> 'The gold or silvery appearance responsible for
> the popular names these ferns bear, is produced in
> various ways. Usually it is due to the secretion of a
> powdery substance that evenly coats the under
> surface of the fronds. Sometimes . . .'

I didn't read on. It did not seem to matter to what
strange caprice of Nature the gold or silver might be
due. It was enough that magic was at work. And it
was a magic that had to be explored.

The deeper I delved into this book, the more fascinating were the revelations it held. For instance, it stated
that 'among ferns will be found a wealth of colour which
will compare favourably with that found even in the
flowering plants of the West Indies'. This statement, in
the light of later experience, has proved to be misleading.
The colour of ferns can in no way be compared with the
colour of flowers, West Indian or otherwise. Both flower
and fern suffers by such a comparison. It is enough to
say that the colour range of ferns is wide and full of
exquisite subtlety, and to leave it at that.

I also learned of the existence of climbing ferns, and
of the large family of 'Filmies', ferns so transparent that
the smallest type can be read through their foliage. Of the
endless variety of frills and borderings which the fern

affect, as though they employed in their service a million tiny milliners with green-gloved fingers. Of the many curious places in which they will grow, the unlikely surfaces which they choose to grace. As for the things I learned about their *vie de cœur*, and the romance with which they brought their children into the world ... only the pen of a Maeterlinck could describe them.

§III

So that was the first step. I was enchanted — in theory. And there, for a little while, it remained. So many other things were happening, not only in my own little world, but in Europe, that there was no time to spare for starting a collection.

However, things calmed down again, and there was no longer any excuse for waiting. But even then I might have hesitated, had chance not taken me to the Fern House at Kew, where I met my first *gymnogramme*. (It sounds rather as if I had encountered a female acrobat hanging from the roof in a pot. But it was not at all like that.)

It was Hitler who drove me to Kew, on that particular day. Or was it Mussolini? I forget. Somebody like that, at any rate, somebody who was making an awful uproar in Central Europe. I wanted to walk about under very big tall trees, in the quiet, and look up into their branches and let their untroubled wisdom sink into me.

So off I went. Usually I set out straight for the beech-woods on arriving at Kew. You very seldom see anybody else there, and they are beautiful at all times of the year ... perhaps even more beautiful in winter than in spring, for it is then that they pin on those small satin waistcoats of dazzling green moss. But just as I was about to visit them, I thought it would be a good idea to go and visit the fernery first, to see what sort of temperature was necessary for what sort of fern. And also, to be frank, to see what sort of fern there *was*.

I turned up the path to the left, and after a minute's walk found myself by the house for semi-tropical ferns. On opening the door, and entering the moist, warm atmosphere, I thought that perhaps there could be found no place in the world more fragrant, more green, and more peaceful. There were no other visitors in the great house at all — only a gardener with a watering-can, in the far corner. The crowd is never attracted by the ferns. The crowd likes the bright gaudy things. For every fifty people who go to see the orchids, only one goes to see the ferns.

For a little while I wandered about, and I remember saying to myself, more than once, 'Well, I *must* say ...' which may not have been a very brilliant remark, but was expressive of a growing appreciation, not unmingled with surprise, at the number of strange and charming plants that kept presenting themselves.

Then, my shoe-lace came undone. If it hadn't come undone, it is possible that these words would not have been written. For I was standing just opposite a *gymno-gramme sulphurea*, and as I stooped to tie the lace, I happened to glance upwards. And the under-side of this fern was thickly coated with gold, pure gold, that glistened in the sunlight.

Perhaps it may sound silly to say that it was the loveliest thing that has ever come my way since I have seen life through the eyes of a gardener. There are so many things you might say that about — your first bunch of the rose called Night (with petals of black velvet on which blood has been spilt) — your first mass of Russell lupins in the sunlight, as gay as a carnival — the first time you walk through an orchard of lemon trees, under a Southern moon. Oh! . . . one might go on for ever like that! But no other single plant nor flower, no orchid certainly, nor even any spray of pear-blossom or plume of lilac, has made me stand in greater wonder before the genius of Nature than this golden fern.

I knelt down before it. The closer I came, the more lovely did the fern appear. There were no half-measures about the gold-dust with which it was so richly coated. It wasn't just a yellow powder. It bore no sort of resemblance to the ochre make-up with which the lily is adorned. Nor was the gold dusted merely here and there — it covered every curve and every crevice of every frond.

The tiny shoots that were springing from the base were, if possible, even brighter. Since their leaves had not yet opened, and there was no green about them, they looked like delicate golden ornaments, daintily disposed round the parent plant.

It was a masterpiece before which Benvenuto Cellini would have stood abashed.

And by the side of it was another excitement. A silver fern! As thickly coated with the metal of the moon as the other had been coated with the metal of the sun. If I had not realized the futility of comparisons at such a moment as this, I would have dared to suggest that the silver fern was even more beautiful than the golden. For it seemed actually luminous with this magic dust. And again, there were no half-measures. It *was* silver. Not just white or grey, not in the least like the leaf, say, of a centaurea. It was silver, hall-marked, pure and glistening from the inexhaustible mint of Nature.

§ I V

I left Kew so thoroughly 'sold' on ferns that even before reaching home I had made a great decision. The domed greenhouse should be given over to them entirely. It would obviously be impossible to put such exquisite creatures as the gold and silver ferns in a converted toolshed; it would be like parking a princess in the pantry. Besides, these ferns would need a certain amount of heat, and there was no adequate means of heating the toolshed.

'Really!' I thought to myself, as I got out of the car,

'The decisions one is making! The swiftness with which life is moving! The gigantic enterprises which are under-taken, day by day!' I felt almost as Hitler must feel, when he decides, in the interval between lunch and tea, to 'protect' another independent republic with the hos-pitable arms of the Reich.

For it *was* a great decision. It meant, for one thing, giving up the bougainvillaea. Or did it? Yes, I am afraid it did. But there would be wonderful consolations. Nothing, for instance, could have been more delightful than the climbing ferns at Kew. I could have them instead of the bougainvillaea. The name of one which I had noted was *Lygodium palmatum*, and it had strange, palm-shaped leaves at the bottom and the most delicate fronds higher up, like pale green feathers. It would be a wrench, denying myself the bougainvillaea, but that dazzling colour would be too hard on the softer, subtler tints of the ferns.

After all, it wasn't as if I should be denying myself *colour*. Indeed, it was through their colours that I had come to love the ferns. And. though it is anticipating, you should be told here and now that one of the most delicious experiences you will ever have in your life is when you invest in your first group of adiantums, such as *A. elegans*, *cuneatum*, *Weigandii* and *chilense*. These are miniature varieties of the common maidenhair (to put it very roughly) but they have heaps of endearing pe-culiarities, and some of them are so thickly embroidered on the underside with tiny spores, that through a magnifying glass they look like the most elaborate satin brocade that ever graced the Court of Louis XVI. But the exciting thing about them is not the intricacy of the craftsmanship that has gone to their making. No. The real thrill is in the colour they turn in autumn. For here, on a diminished scale, is all the beauty of the woods at fall . . . the scarlets and the buffs, the crimsons, the fawns, and the spectral yellows.

It is all a question of stepping, mentally, into the shoes of Gulliver on his visit to Lilliput. I have, in all, eighteen of these ferns, and the space they occupy on the shelf cannot be much more than four feet. On an October morning, when the early sun is shining through the glass (they like the early sun in autumn), I can go down to the greenhouse, shut the door, look up at the little shelf, and become Gulliver in an instant. Then, it is no longer a row of ferns; it is a great wood, with massive branches, through which the sunshine filters in a hundred glowing shades. For the leaves are turning . . . the great green spaces are lit with fires of gold and red. A whole hour you may wander thus, walking in the wood which is four feet long, climbing the trees whose trunks you might snip off with a pair of nail-scissors.

Yes, it is a great thing, this Gulliver business. And in view of the present state of the world, it looks as though we may all have to cultivate it, with increasing concentration as the years speed by.

§ v

It would not be practical to write at any great length about the ferns, because even for the keenest gardener it is a pretty technical business. It is only necessary to give you a few important hints.

The first is that you must not be lured, by my enthusiasm, into investing in a whole lot of ferns unless you are one of those people who really like watering. (Or unless, of course, you have a delicate-fingered member of your household who can be spared from his or her job for at least twenty minutes twice a day all the year round.) Personally I adore watering. It seems such a *hospitable* thing to do. To stand, like God, above all that waving, trembling green, to pour down streams of life-giving fluid, to hear the drip, drip of the water on the floor, to note the gratitude of the recipients — what could be more delightful? It sets one up for the whole day. However, if you don't feel like that, you must be left to wallow in your own sordid ways, alone.

The next thing is about the house itself. It is very difficult here not to lapse into the jargon of gardening textbooks (which might be a relief to some people, after all these adjectives).

There are three things to remember about the house. The first is very nice and encouraging, namely, that you don't want a lot of light. My own house, in spite of the thick glass of the dome, and in spite of the fact that there is only one window, is really too light, and has to be shaded in the summer. This means that you can have a fernery in the most unlikely places, in the gloomiest backyard, on a lighthouse, by the side of the docks. You might even have a fernery in the shadow of a Wall Street brokerage house, which would be a much better investment than most that you are likely to make in that repellant thoroughfare.

Secondly, about the house, you *must* be able to heat it adequately. However, we went into all that in a previous chapter. The only reason I mention it again is because you might think of going in for ferns that needed little or no heat. There are plenty of them, and very beautiful they are. But since the love of ferns is, to a certain extent, an acquired taste (though how easily acquired, you would never guess), it is a little risky to limit yourself to the more ordinary varieties. You might — let's face it — be bored.

Thirdly, still about the house, do begin at once to make plans to have things growing in beds or out of walls or in niches, and not only in pots. You want to feel that the whole *house* is living, that it is a miraculous nest of green, that the very walls are fertile. The difference between a plant in a pot and a plant in the soil is the difference between a man in an hotel and a man in his own home.

There are all sorts of ways in which you can escape being pot-bound. You can have beds all along the sides under the shelves. They need only be about three inches deep, but as long as they are drained, they will give nourishment to ferns that will climb up to the roof, and also to ferns that will wander about on the earth, and clamber over the edge, and generally disport themselves in the prettiest manner.

There are various other ways to avoid this pot-bound feeling . . . (I wish that didn't sound so like a treatise on indigestion). My own greenhouse is such a peculiar shape that perhaps I have an unfair advantage in this respect. There are so many corners that can be boxed in and planted, so many odd bays and jutting-out pieces that can be amusingly treated. And all round the roof there is a little trough which is filled with *Selaginella uncinata*. This hangs down in charming festoons and makes you feel you are in the jungle.

Needless to say, the majority of your ferns will *have* to be in pots, but as long as you get enough of the other sort it won't matter so much. And whatever else you have there are three things on which I really do insist. One is the above-mentioned *Selaginella uncinata*. Believe it or not, it is a *blue* fern. Well, if you must be tiresomely accurate, blue *and* green, although the blue bits are as blue as a turquoise. This loves being taken out of its pot and put into some sort of niche. It is a charming, trailing affair, that looks very vague, and does not seem to be able to make up its mind where it wants to go to. But as it is so delightful, you do not mind, and let it have its own sweet way.

The next essential is *Selaginella Brownii*. This doesn't look like a fern at all. (A great many ferns don't.) It looks like the most gorgeous moss you ever saw, the sort of moss that you find on the trunk of a fallen tree, by the side of a river, in November. If you get several pots of this, you can plant them near each other so that they can join up. They need an enormous amount of water. And when you are watering them, if you happen to be in a Gulliver mood, you can pretend you are in the middle of them, caught in a treacherous swamp, and have an awful five minutes trying to get out.

The last essential is *Platycerium alcicorne*. I could write a long botanical treatise on why this is a fern, but it would bore you as much as it would bore me, and anyway you would never believe it. For it looks even less like a fern than *Selaginella Brownii*. It looks exactly like the sort of hats that royalty wore in the days of Edward VII. . . . indeed, if you put a group of them together, and photographed them from the rear, you could call it, 'Behind the Royal Box at Ascot, 1911'. But apart from the fact that they are so comic — (And I don't see why you shouldn't allow Nature a sense of humour) — they are also admirably behaved. When you transplant them, you can get them to cling like leeches to a piece of cork. You can dispose them all over the place, and they give an effect of great luxury and curiousness. In fact, I have rather insulted them by saying that they are comic. Properly arranged, you would say they were great moths, sleeping high up among a protective environment of green.

§ VI

And now, what was that last thing to tell you about ferns? Oh, yes. How to begin.

Personally I feel very strongly that you must put the cart before the horse, and a buy a collection before you know anything about them. It can be as tiny as you like or as large as you can afford, but until the ferns are actually there, under your eyes, demanding admiration, you will only dither about with a lot of books, wondering what to get, and why, and how. You could spend many years learning the infinite variations of even one family of ferns, and life is too short for that.

But you must do a *little* work on them. You mustn't fool yourself with the idea that it's going to be as simple as telling the difference between, say, an *Etoile de Hollande* and a *Lord Kitchener*, between an *Ophelia* and a *Frau Karl Druschki*. It's not baby work. You must begin by learning the main branches, and after that you *must* learn the principal names of these branches. And the names are, quite frankly, appalling. Americans, who have a genius for names, and who can and do repeat, with fierce accuracy, the most exotic cognomens of persons they meet at the noisiest party, may not find it so difficult. But the British, who purposely deafen themselves when introductions are being made, will be so discouraged that they may decide to give up the whole thing as a bad job.

I am so determined that you should *not* give it up, that I am going to let you into the secret of a way in which these names can be made a little less difficult. It is a sort of game, in which you associate the names with other things more familiar to you.

Supposing we give you some examples.

Asplenium lunulatum. This, of course, instantly conjures up the pictures of a donkey coming home late, in the moonlight, because it has eaten too much. Or does it? Well, to me it does, at any rate. I should have thought it was simple enough. *As.* That's the donkey. *Plenium.* Suggestive of repletion. *Lunulatum.* Coming home late in the moonlight.

If this is too difficult, try another. *Doodia aspera.* Otherwise, 'Darling, do pronounce your h's'.

Take another. *Nothoclaena marantae.* Can the interpretation of this remain for even an instant in obscurity? Does it not immediately suggest a young man persuading his fiancée (by name Laena) to refrain from drinking hock, because his mother disapproves of it? 'Not hock, Laena.' That is what he says. And — being modern and disinclined to long explanations — he does not say, 'My mother disapproves of it, darling.' He just says, 'Ma anti.' *Nothoclaena marantae.* You would have taken weeks to learn that, if it hadn't been for me.

Some of the names are even simpler. *Todea plumosa* is, of course, a female toad about to be presented at Court. *Gymnogramme Wettenhalliana* is, beyond question, a lady acrobat standing in the hall after being caught in a rainstorm. *Anemia rotundifolia* is one of those fat boys in movies about American youth.

It should now be simple for you to learn the names of the ferns, to enjoy their infinite variety and incidentally to cause considerable irritation, by the extent of your learning, in the hearts of a number of your most intimate friends.

CHAPTER XII

THE TRIUMPHS OF LILLIPUT

DURING the whole of that winter I was so often in the fernery that I hardly noticed, outside, the slow paling of the light, the faint misting of the trees, the gradual crescendo of bird-song, that betokened the coming of spring. There were so many things to learn, in the shelter of the glass, and so many things to do. Little ballets to arrange, in which ten green fans fluttered in line. Miniature waterfalls to devise in which the spray was the colour of jade, falling soundlessly, exquisitely, on boulders of cork. Tiny wars to be waged, in which ferns with crests of silver advanced towards ferns with plumes of gold, and in which the prize was always Beauty.

But one day I stepped out into the sunshine, rubbed my eyes, and found that it was spring. And the triangle had blossomed into a garden.

I shall never forget that April. The winter had been so busy that flowers, shrubs and bulbs had been planted in a mad hurry, many of them far too late. I even dug in a cluster of grape hyacinths on Christmas Day! They were already sprouting, and I felt very guilty about treating them in this way, for grape hyacinths ought to be planted the first week in September (whatever the bulb merchants may say). All the same, they came up. They looked a little fatigued, and they were on the pale side, but they did not fail me.

Looking back on it all, it is astonishing to recall the number of experiments which succeeded. As you may gather from the title of this chapter, most of these experiments were on a very small scale. The triumphs were Lilliputian. But we have so often reminded ourselves that every city gardener is a Gulliver at heart, that perhaps you will not mind hearing about them.

Consider the case of the daffodils. In the country at Allways, one of the things to which I always looked forward most eagerly was the sight of the first clumps of daffodils, dancing under the trees in the wood. It is an obvious pleasure, which I share with a great many simple people, but there is no harm in being obvious or simple, if you feel like it. And in this case I feel like it so much that if I were ever struck with blindness, and were told that I might have just one minute to look upon any sight in the world, it would be no human face that I should choose, nor any picture, nor any beloved city. It would be a drift of daffodils, dancing in the April wind, under the trees of Allways.

Obviously, in the garden at Heathstead, one couldn't have anything like this — daffodils and nothing else. It would have meant planting daffodils here, there and everywhere. The little pools of grape hyacinths would have to go, and the clusters of snowdrops, and the *poeticus narcissi* (which always seem to look a more dazzling white in London than anywhere else).

All the same, I did long for that illusion of a real drift of daffodils. And like most of the things I longed for, I got it in the end. Simply by going mad one day, and ordering large quantities of *Narcissus cyclamineus*, which are never more than two inches high.

Before you protest that it is far too expensive for the average gardener, that you have to have a new hat, and that the rates are bound to go up next year, do listen to what happens if you invest in this enchanting flower.

First of all a bag of peanuts arrives at the house. At least, that is what they look like — small, rather dingy peanuts. After you have counted them (because you ordered four hundred, and you cannot believe that there can be so many in such a small bag), you put them carefully away in a drawer, and go out to see where they can be planted.

The ideal place, of course, would be under a very tiny tree. Taking the average height of a *Narcissus cyclamineus* as two inches, and the average height of the ordinary daffodil as sixteen inches, you would need a tree about two or three feet high to get the right effect. If you haven't got such a thing (and I hadn't), you will have to exercise your ingenuity in other ways.

Mine were planted in three or four very carefully arranged drifts at the foot of the two walls which concealed the secret garden. For three reasons.

Firstly, because in this position they could be seen not only from the house, but from every other part of the garden.

Secondly, because it was possible, by being artful in arranging them, to give the effect that they were only the *beginning* of a drift which extended indefinitely behind the centre wall.

Thirdly, because at this place the turf was always in fine condition, well-drained, and unlikely to be disturbed. These bulbs cost about thirty-six shillings a hundred, and when you invest in bulbs at such a price, you expect them to be a permanent investment, a gilt-edged security that will pay you golden dividends year after year.

There are two ways of planting the bulbs. One is to get an old pencil or a skewer, or something like that, and to dig it into the turf for about an inch and a half, dropping a bulb into each hole and covering it up again. This method is not to be recommended. After you have dug the pencil in for about a hundred and ninety-seven times you feel the whole thing is a crashing bore. Also you forget where you put some of the bulbs, and you spear the pencil through those which you have already planted, and bang goes sixpence.

It is far better to plan exactly where you want them to go, down to the last little spur of flowers that is to jut out in delightful irregularity, to mark the grass accordingly, and then to get a sharp knife, and slice off the top turf to a depth, at the very most, of an inch and a half. If you go any deeper, the bulbs will be buried. Then you must clean the soil, take out any large pebbles, and arrange the bulbs as you desire, planting them very close together.

There are few things in life more pleasant, and of all my experiments in the Gulliver vein, this was one of the most successful. From my window the daffodils looked as though some amiable spirit had poured out two heaps of golden sovereigns during the night, scattered them over the grass, and departed. But when you go out, approach them, kneel down by them, and get into the Gulliver mood, they . . . well, they *are* a drift of daffodils, real daffodils. You forget the rest of the world, forget the wall that towers gigantically over your head. You forget it so completely that if a kitten were suddenly to run into the picture, you would start back in horror, convinced that it was a rhinoceros.

§ 11

That was the first triumph of Gulliver.

The next concerns the old question of Design.

The triangle was a thing of the past, but the garden was still haunted by its ghost. You would have been haunted too, if you had lived for months with that sharp apex boring into your brain. Besides, although the wretched thing was slain, it was only slain in theory. The brick frame was all right, but how would it look when it was filled with flowers? Was it not possible that a design which hung on so delicate a balance might once more be upset?

As soon as most of the spring flowers were out it became apparent that it *was* possible for the design to be upset. Not so seriously as to cause positive distress, but enough to be worrying. You see, in my passion to bring the Eye round to the left, I had planted a bold cluster of *poeticus Narcissi* in the extreme left-hand corner, and since these were not only in deep shade but in a soil which had been inadequately drained, a number of them rotted. What should have been a dazzling mass of white became only a feeble blur. So the Eye, the intolerably vagrant Eye, fastened upon the more abundant Narcissi in the *centre*. And the ghost of the triangle rose from its distant grave.

This was a battle that had to be fought. It had to be fought with mechanical, rather than floral weapons, because that little corner to which the Eye must be guided was too dark and damp to be relied upon to produce any very brilliant blossoms.

So once more, I sat down and thought. How to bring the Eye round to the left. I retraced all the steps that we had taken to date. The path, of course, had been a great advance. The Eye naturally followed it to its conclusion at the extreme left side of the terrace. The centre wall had been indispensable, and now that the lilacs were planted in the left-hand corner, and the camellia tree was peering over the top, the Eye could not resist giving these things their due attention. But it still wanted one or two definite spots of light or colour to which the Eye would be attracted. The composition *demanded* it. Whence were the spots to come?

Sometimes ... so urgent was the need of bringing round the Eye that I almost wished that the House-Next-Door would be leased to some tall and striking female who would spend a large portion of her life on her lawn, dressed in dazzling colours, waving her arms over her head. That would bring the Eye round all right. Particularly if, every time she saw anyone emerge from the door, she drew attention to herself by loud and distressful screams. But there seemed no chance of such a person joining our community. Only a shady lawn, on which the birds darted about — a lawn which rarely saw the shadow of its owner.

One day, in order to see where the 'high spots' in the composition were needed, I experimented by placing white jugs at intervals along the wall. Needless to say, Mrs. H. found this an occasion for ascending to her bedroom window and glowering out to see what was happening. What she thought was afoot, it would be difficult to say. People do not put white jugs on the wall without some reason, but what could that reason be? It may be gathered that I rather like doing things which mystify Mrs. H. Anyway, this time she couldn't complain about Ancient Lights.

No sooner were the jugs in position — one in a line with the terrace, one by the camellia, and one perched on the left-hand ledge of the greenhouse, under the dome — than I knew exactly what was needed. Those white pigeons that I had seen in an old shop off Brompton Square! They were charming creatures. They looked

so like real pigeons that I had gone in to ask about them.
They were French, covered with a thick glaze, and they
were so expensive that I hadn't thought myself justified
in buying them for the inside of the house. But now, the
white jugs had proved that the pigeons could no longer
be regarded as a luxury. They were a stern necessity.
Without a moment's delay I put on my hat and sped towards Brompton Square, praying that London might
not be too pigeon-conscious on this afternoon. Within an
hour I was back again, carrying three stern necessities
under my arm. One pouting, one spreading its tail, and
one with wings outstretched.

As a general rule, I don't like garden ornaments.
Somewhere, we may be sure, in one of the suburbs of
Purgatory, there is an arid garden where dwell the
spirits of all those misshapen creatures who have been
decorating so many gardens for so many years. In this
strange hell the traveller will see bloated cupids, staggering with leaden feet down pavements for which the
word 'crazy' would be an understatement. They will see
fearsome plaster girls who, as they pass by, spout a
mouthful of water from between their cracked lips.
Through the upper airs glazed pelicans will flap, back
and forth, pretending to be decorative, when all the
time they know that they are evil spirits.

But these pigeons were different. You really *must*
agree that they were different, if you look at the photograph which shows them. It would worry me if you were
not pro-pigeon. So far, there has been only one person in

the anti-pigeon camp, and she is Mrs. H., and a sense of the elementary decencies ought to prevent you from wishing to be associated with *her*.

You must also agree that they definitely bring the Eye round to the left. When you step out on to the terrace

they are almost the first things the Eye observes, for they are washed every week and are always bright and glistening. The Eye rests upon them with pleasure. Sometimes, indeed, it does more than that . . . it endows them with life, and flutters their feathers. And sends them in imagination on enchanted journeys, high up over the tree-tops, three flecks of white against the blue, with the sunlight glistening on their wings.

§ III

That, you must admit, was a Gulliver triumph, for surely in no gardens but those of Lilliput could the whole fragrant fabric be dependent upon the outstretched wing of a white bird, and an artificial bird at that.

However, in case this device is too fanciful for your taste, you will learn with relief that the next triumph was of a sternly practical nature — one in which you can share yourself if you are so inclined.

To tell of it, the clock must be set forward six months, but please try to remember that for all practical purposes we are still in the second spring of the garden. At least, that is the date to which we must return after this tale is told.

One day in October (that is to say, six months ahead of where we are now) I was walking round the garden, wondering for the hundredth time where I could 'squeeze something in'.

The something in this case was a paeony, or rather three paeonies, one pink, one crimson, and one white. They had gone down on the garden list during the previous June, because I had noticed that the paeonies in the House-Next-Door were as fine as any I had ever seen.

I walked round and round, wondering whether to scoop out yet another foot of lawn here, or juggle with a bit of turf there. It was hopeless. The lawn (as it was continually necessary to remind oneself) was sacrosanct. An inch smaller, and it would cease to be a lawn at all; it would look like a map of Poland after the third Partition. So what was one to do?

I sat down, chewed a bit of grass, and concentrated.

After a little while one conclusion presented itself, namely, that if the garden was to be developed any more there was only one direction in which such a development could possibly take place — towards the sky. This might bring one into argument with the London County Council.

But sitting there, with the blank in front, I began to see light. For I was sitting immediately opposite a bed which would have been ideal for the paeonies, had it not been for the fact that it had already been apportioned to wallflowers next spring and antirrhinums next summer. Remembering these two flowers, I recollected that they both took kindly to walls, that they had a genius which could extract a living from the barest necessities of existence. Why not therefore use the wall for these flowers, and allow the paeonies to luxuriate in their rich bed, all alone?

It was not, however, quite as simple as that.

There were several reasons why it was impracticable to attempt to grow flowers on the top of the wall. There were, in fact, seventeen reasons, some black, some tabby and two ginger. It would obviously be the act of a cad and a barbarian to interfere with the thoroughfares which the cats of the neighbourhood were so gracious as to use — (though in the past I had been guilty, to a minor degree, of feeble attempts to discourage them). And even if it had not been caddish, it would have been absurd. For few things are so fascinating, so calculated to brighten up one's day, as the sight of a slim and elegant creature in black, walking down a wall with the delicacy of Agag, pausing to look at nothing, every muscle tense, and then, with a grace which must be the despair of ballet dancers, leaping into the next door garden, arrogantly, effortlessly, as though the only reason why it did not fly was because flying was a little vulgar.

But it would have been difficult to grow flowers in a new wall, even if one's respect for the sacred rights of cats had permitted the attempt. Apart from the fact that a new wall takes a lot of chipping, and looks unsightly when it has been chipped, it seems to contain a number of chemicals which most flowers heartily dislike. And though you may strike a lucky patch, and manage to get something to survive in a pocket of soil, the problem of draining is almost insuperable. Either the drainage is too efficient, so that half the earth runs away, leaving the plant to starve, or it is not efficient enough, and the roots rot in stagnant water.

It takes a very old wall, wrinkled by a thousand rains and winds, enriched by a thousand chance particles of matter, of dust and flying leaf, to offer a shelter in which a flower can really feel at home. Even then, how infinite must have been the number of seeds that have drifted into it, on a summer breeze, before a single one found a resting place . . . seeds from sleepy wallflowers, and from sun-drenched poppies, seeds from the tall valerians, and from the baby snapdragons in the pavement's crevice.

had to be solemnly trimmed with nail scissors. About a border five feet long which contained so many varieties of plants that part of it was treated with lime, part with ammonium sulphate, and part with bone-meal. And never were the three allowed to meet!

I am afraid I became almost morbid about it. Like Gulliver who, when he returned to the real world, staggered back from his wife under the impression that she was a giantess. I found myself avoiding tall people, large houses, great trees. Conversely I could not go to a party and see anything undersized in females without thinking how well she would look walking down the new garden path. Her feet would not spread out on to the grass, the top of her hat would hardly come up to the first branch of the may tree, and if you made her stand beneath the dome (which you certainly would), you could photograph her and call it 'Orphan child looking at St. Paul's'.

I couldn't bear large women in the garden — unless they were lying down, foreshortened, with their feet to the north. But though it may seem strange, the number of really large women who, on entering the garden, can be relied upon to lie down in such a manner without asking any pointed question is definitely and perhaps mercifully, limited.

And so for some little while a quite new collection of visitors, all midgets, began to be invited to lunch. As I watched them sitting there, I sometimes thought how awful it would be if they suddenly realized that they had been invited, not for their wit nor for their beauty, but for the extent to which they approximated to the proportions of dwarfs. However, when they trotted round the garden after lunch, the sight of them was so pleasant that I felt quite affectionate.

CHAPTER XIII

BIGGER AND BIGGER

THERE are several minor differences — apart from the major matter of the moustache — which distinguish me from Herr Hitler, and one of them is the fact that I have learnt how to enlarge my territory without going outside my own boundaries.

For a Nazi, the enlargement of the garden would have been a very simple matter. Firstly he would have gone out on to the lawn, and made loud noises about the lack of 'breathing space'. On the next day he would have purchased a megaphone, obtained the assistance of Gaskin, and made even louder noises. On the third day he would have gone out at twilight with a hammer, hit the Lady-Next-Door on the head, knocked down the wall, and announced that honour was now appeased and that his territorial ambitions in Heathstead were at an end.

A week later, however, he would have gone out once more on to the lawn, and made more noises, this time in the direction of Mrs. H. He would have proclaimed in agonized tones that Rose and Cavalier had been rudely chased off Mrs. H.'s herbaceous border, that this was an intolerable 'affront', and that he could not rest until his 'brethren', of almost pure Siamese blood, were no longer 'tortured'. He would then have climbed on to the dome with a hose-pipe, squirted Mrs. H. out of existence, and annexed her garden too. Life, for a dictator, must be almost too simple to be fun.

However, not being a dictator, I had to use brains instead of brawn. And though it seems incredible, the title of this chapter is a sober statement of fact. The garden *was* getting bigger and bigger.

During the spring and summer, admittedly, it remained comparatively quiescent. There was much rushing backwards and forwards with plants, much sowing of seeds, and many minor encroachments on the lawn, three inches here, six inches there. But there were no major annexations. It was not till the autumn (i.e. the beginning of the second year) that the real developments began.

And then the garden suddenly became almost twice the size.

I am not being 'whimsical'. It was not a question of fairies arriving in the middle of the night, waving magic wands, and causing the walls to glide outwards — though if there were an agency where such creatures could be hired, I should employ them with the greatest satisfaction. The result may have looked like magic, but there was no illusion about it. The expansion which is about to be described was the result of hard work and hard thinking.

It began at the left-hand end of the terrace. So far we have not halted there. We have only walked dutifully to the wall, turned right, and proceeded down the garden path. But it is time that we paused, for this corner is the scene of the next advance.

It is a pity that no photograph was taken of that corner before it was transformed. It was so exceptionally dingy. The garden wall conducted to the edge of the House-Next-Door, and then ... well, there, there was just a square space with a wooden fence that shut off the door of the kitchen. In the middle of this space was an old bush of privet, which I had not yet had the heart to cut down. The whole thing looked something like this:

Not very attractive, you will agree. It looked particularly unpleasant through the french window of the dining-room.

But what was to be done with it? Only one side of it got the sun. It was dripped upon from all directions. It was just a dark, damp gap; at least, that was what it seemed. Even Rose and Cavalier, who could be counted on to explore everything, very seldom entered it. Sometimes they would hurry in, on one of their tours of inspection, give the privet a single disdainful sniff, and then hurry out again. But that was all.

So on the principle that one change leads to another — a principle which had never yet failed to produce results — I cut down the privet.

Needless to say, Mrs. H. was in on this. Just as the last drab and straggly branch had been dragged out into the drive, she emerged from her front door with a letter she was taking to the post, a letter which I am convinced she had written in order to give her an excuse to go out. She hurried along, a bright smile on her face, not 'seeing' the privet. Then suddenly she 'saw' it. The smile faded. She flinched. A carefully modulated expression of distress, wistfulness and outraged sensibility appeared on her face. It was as much as she could do, you would say, to force even the feeblest smile.

'Good morning, Mrs. H.,' I called, just as she was passing.

She turned. In a very faint voice she said, 'Good morning'. She looked over my head. She was far, far too sensitive to look at the slaughtered privet.

'What a lovely morning.'

For some of us . . .' and here she permitted herself a momentary glance . . . 'I expect it is.' With which, she departed.

Well, I thought, at least she is beginning to be tamed a

little. There was a time when she would have bounced into the house and demanded in shrill tones how I had the effrontery to cut down 'her' beautiful privet. And though she was tiresome as a martyr, she was even more so as an aggressor.

The pillar box is only at the top of the road, and in a few minutes Mrs. H.'s footsteps once more echoed down the drive. Not wishing to continue a profitless argument, I turned my back and pretended to busy myself with the privet.

The footsteps stopped, just behind me. There was the sound of a throat being cleared in a mournful but lady-like manner. I turned round. It was Mrs. H., and she was gazing at the privet.

'I wonder,' she inquired meekly, 'might I have just a tiny branch?'

'Of the privet, Mrs. H.? Of course. But if you were thinking of taking cuttings, I'm afraid . . .'

She shook her head. 'Oh, no. I know there's no chance of *that*. Too late.' She sighed, heavily. 'Just to have in the house. Something green.'

Whatever else the privet might have been, it was not green, but I let that pass. I took out the secateurs and searched for a branch that was not quite so ill-shaped as the rest. While I was doing so, Mrs. H. continued.

'Terrible,' she said, as if she were speaking to herself, 'when we have to do these things. Taking life. Destroying. However . . .' She paused. 'Oh, *please!*'

'It's no trouble, Mrs. H.'

'Oh, *please!*' She saw that I had just stripped off a particularly hideous branch, and was about to throw it in the mud. She extended her gloved hand. 'Might I?' in a pleading voice.

'It's very dirty.'

She shook her head. Well, if she wanted to ruin her gloves just to annoy me, she was welcome.

She took the privet, and stood there holding it, gazing at it as though it were an object of exquisite beauty.

'Such an old friend,' she breathed.

Now this was too much. Unless Mrs. H. had climbed up on my roof, and lain on her stomach, gazing over the edge, she had never even *seen* the privet.

'I beg your pardon?'

She waved her hand vaguely at the surrounding shrubs. 'Old friends,' she said. 'All these trees, these green things.' And added, in somewhat sharper tones, 'What is left of them.'

'I see.' I snipped off the branch. 'I thought you meant that this privet was an old friend. But of course, you've never seen it before.'

'To me . . . all green things . . . old friends.'

'This isn't very green, Mrs. H.' — (snip, snip) — 'but I'm afraid it's the best I can do' — (snip, snip!) — 'So if you like to take it . . .' I held out a bunch that was large enough to form a fair-sized bonfire, and thrust it into her arms. It was an impolite action, but it did me good. And Mrs. H., in the circumstances, could not protest. She *had* to clasp the privet to her arms. She *had* to check the expression of alarm and disgust which she naturally felt when she saw the black smudges it was making all over her dress. She *had* to force a look of tenderness, of protection. She *had* to hurry away, and get rid of the wretched stuff before her dress was ruined.

That round, you must admit, was definitely in my favour.

§ 11

It was another woman who, some weeks later, gave a fresh twist to the comedy.

After the privet had departed, the little space it had occupied seemed less confined and the dining-room less gloomy. After the outside walls had been whitewashed, it became almost bright. But it was still ugly and purposeless; it was still *wasted*. That was the real worry; the waste when every other inch of the land was serving some useful object.

One dreary November day, Héloise came to lunch. She had a cold; I had a headache; the fog was so thick in the city that she was three-quarters of an hour late and the lunch was burned to ashes — but oh, how *glad* she was about it all.

After lunch she said that she would like to see the garden. (Clasping her hands, and gazing wide-eyed at a lot of nothing.)

'No, Héloise. Your cold is too bad.'

She replied, nasally, that this was of no account.

'There's nothing to see, anyway.'

With mock-horror, she advanced towards me. *Very* wide-eyed, she was, at that moment. She made a motion of putting her forefinger to my lip, and possibly would have done so, had not my expression indicated that I might bite it.

'For *you* to say that!' she cried. 'You know there's always something to see in a *garden*!'

'Yes,' I snapped. 'But I've seen it.'

'But I haven't. And I want to be shown.'

Checking a groan, I helped her on with her coat, much to the disgust of Cavalier, who had made himself a nest in it. We went outside. It looked dreary beyond belief. The fog was drifting up from the city, and the atmosphere was pale ochre. Nevertheless, Héloise continued to be glad.

'What atmosphere!' she breathed. 'If only I could paint!' She tripped to the end of the terrace. 'The trees look like ghosts,' she continued, 'and the little dome — you would say it was floating.' She narrowed her eyes, painting in imagination. 'The palest yellows and very misty mauves . . . that's what it wants.'

'Soap and water is what it'll want, if this fog goes on.'

She tinkled gaily and turned round, looking in the direction of the wasted corner.

'Wretched, isn't it?' I said.

'Wretched? What?'

'That old corner. It's not so bad now it's whitewashed, but it's still pretty awful. Nothing to be done about it, though. I've thought and thought.'

'But you needn't see it. *I* don't see it.'

'You're looking straight at it, at this moment.'

'Yes. But I don't *see* it.' She spoke in terms of the loftiest idealism. She touched her forehead with her finger. 'I don't see it *here*.'

'Then you should take more water with it, Héloise.' (She likes being insulted, that girl.)

Another gay tinkle. A step forward. Ah . . . she did see it, this time! And having seen it, she said something quite idiotic.

'But of course,' she cried. 'A *loggia*!'

'Where?'

'There! It's the very place. A little roof. Two little walls. A little pillar.'

'*Much* more water with it, Héloise.'

'And you'll be able to paint the inside a heavenly Italian pink, and sit under the little arch in a dressing gown, meditating.'

It seemed to me at the time, and it must seem to you now, a nauseating prospect, both for me and for anybody who might chance to pass by. I said so. However, no arguments could damp her enthusiasm, and finally, to close the subject, I took her out and treated her to a movie.

§ III

But the subject was not closed. Weak as it may sound, feeble as you may think me, I could not get Héloise's suggestion out of my head.

If only she had not used the word '*loggia*'! A *loggia* in the suburb of Heathstead! It set the teeth on edge, that word, in such a context. It made me think of the people who speak of their courtyards as '*patios*', who call luncheon '*tiffin*', and champagne 'bubbly'. It had the same gross incongruity as the word 'Casino' when applied to those draughty erections on the south coast of England in which holiday-makers sit around drinking tea to the accompaniment of a female string band. It even reminded me of a dreadful woman in Wiltshire who refers to her swimming pool (which is usually empty, and quite inadequate anyway) as '*la piscine*'. Not *the* piscine, I ask you! *La*! She goes the whole hog.

But gradually it began to seem rather childish to be deterred like this, just by a word. Loggia or no loggia, one could make a charming little place there. A sort of outside room. All that was needed was to build a wall at the back, instead of the wooden fence, another wall to hide the House-Next-Door, a tiled roof, and there you were! The front, looking out on to the terrace, would be arched, with a small arched window. And although it was a pity that Héloise had been the one to suggest it, the inside would have to be painted that gay, warm Italian pink, which is, of all colours, the colour of love.

(Just to spite Héloise, I decided always to refer to it, in her presence, as 'the orangery'.)

Anyway, it must be done. Once more Mr. Peregrine was summoned, once more the drive was cluttered up with lorries, once more Mrs. H.'s life was made a misery — but the loggia was built.

Though I say it myself, it was a pretty place. It was in complete harmony with the architecture of the rest of the house, in spite of the Italian character of the little pilaster which supported one side of the arched window.

And it was to lead to great adventures, to a whole new chapter in my gardening life.

But it is too early to tell of those adventures just yet. For meanwhile, the garden was growing fast, in several other directions.

§ I V

One of the strangest things about man is his infinite capacity for not noticing things. Most of us are humiliated when we try to solve the simplest competitions designed to test our powers of observation. How many steps are there before your front-door? The Grand Lama of Thibet is probably as well-informed. How many teeth do you possess? Heaven alone knows. Far too many, judging from the dentist's bills. What is the exact date on which your driving licence expires? It would be easier to tell the date of Hitler's birthday. Nobody in Europe is ever allowed to forget *that*.

Thus it was, on the occasion of the new herbaceous border. (Yes, we are actually going to create one now!) Somebody said to me, after looking round the garden, 'But what a pity you haven't got any roses.'

'No roses?' I exclaimed. 'What are you talking about? There's a *Gloire de Dijon*, and an *Etoile de Hollande*, and a *Souvenir de Claudius Denouyel*. No roses! I have three!'

'Yes, but they're all climbers. I meant ordinary roses and half-standards, and that sort of thing.'

'You can't have everything,' I replied, rather shortly. 'I should like a cedar of Lebanon and a trout-stream, but one has to practise self-denial in the city.'

'All the same,' she said blandly, 'I think it's funny that you haven't any. I should have thought you would have missed them.'

Maddening woman! As if I didn't miss them, week in and week out! I tried to forget what she had said, but to no purpose. I *had* to have some roses, particularly half-standards, which are so ideal for cutting. But where?

Where, oh where?

For days I wandered about, searching for a place. Then suddenly I found it. A whole new bed, capable of taking at least a dozen roses, and a great deal of new herbaceous stuff as well.

Hence the mention of man's infinite capacity for not

noticing things. For the new bed, was, if you please, under my very nose, on the terrace itself!

You may remember that in the plan of the garden, on page 104, there are two small beds against the house, one beneath the study window, and one beneath the window of the dining-room. These beds were not only very small, but the soil in them was always parched, because the eaves kept off all the rain. In spite of this, things didn't do so badly in them. In the first year we had quite a show of Russell lupins, and one or two fine delphiniums. There were some good hardy chrysanthemums, too, in the autumn.

Why hadn't I thought of these beds before? Because I didn't want to spoil the terrace, I suppose. But the terrace was out of all proportion to the rest of the garden. True, it wasn't comparable to the House of Lords, but at least four people could walk abreast on it, which was more than you could say for any other part, except the lawn. Why should four people walk abreast on my terrace? It would only be disturbing. Without delay, I went out to the toolshed, got a pick, and began hacking away at the big square stones.

They came up easily. Within an hour the bed under the dining-room window had become four times as large as it had been before. It was now — well, a *bed*. Something really respectable, stretching a long way out beyond the shelter of the roof, in full sunlight. The biggest bed in the whole garden. Sitting under my very nose for nearly three years!

To my great delight, the terrace wasn't spoilt. Though four people might no longer be able to walk abreast on it, two could. And two people, in a garden, is just about the right number.

§ v

Now that at last there was a real bed, I suppose that for the sake of the story I ought to tell you that I did something very sensational in it, filling it with all sorts of things that you have never heard of, achieving results of surpassing magnificence.

I did nothing of the kind. I just got twelve half-standard roses and planted them in a line along the edge. Then, underneath the roses, a border of catmint. In the left-hand corner a group of Russell lupins, next to a group of delphiniums. At the back a cluster of Michaelmas daisies and early chrysanthemums. In front of that a group of phlox, and six columbines. In the far corner, a cluster of Mrs. Sinkins pinks, with the contents of a penny packet of sweet sultans scattered in between.

What could be more obvious? Nothing. What could be more delightful? Nothing. It is all very well to go in for exotics, but you *must* have the obvious things first. How can a garden be called a garden if these old favourites are not to be found in it? And though it sounds incredible, there was still a lot of room in that border for various things which suggested themselves ... usually in the middle of the night.

For example, lavender. Imagine it, forgetting lavender! Out of bed I sprang, and wrote 'Lavender Vital' on a piece of paper, and stuck it up on the looking-glass. By the morning that piece of paper had been decorated with a number of other slogans, such as ...

> Why No Clarkia?
> Candytuft *essential*.
> What about 2 Campanulas?
> Mignonette whatever Happens.
> Geums? Japanese Anemones?

Do you spring out of bed like that, in the middle of the night, in case there is something you may forget? Do you stick up notices like 'Must have a *mass* of grape hyacinths in the drive next year', and tie it round your toothbrush, so that you will put it in your gardening diary first thing in the morning? Maybe it is a purely personal eccentricity. Perhaps I carry it to extremes. One day I nearly went down into the City having forgotten to remove from my hat a large envelope bearing the strange device, 'Have you sprayed *everything*?' It was Gaskin who saved me from this blunder which, as he pointed out, might have been construed by my fellow-passengers as a reflection on their personal daintiness.

But the question I really wanted to ask you is, Do you walk round and round *and* round your garden like this, seeking for some place, even if it be only a few square inches, which can be put to good account? And although you know quite well that there is no place, that it would be utterly impossible to squeeze in even a clump of mint so small that it would hardly produce enough sauce to go with a single lamb chop, do you find, on your thousandth search, that there actually is a place after all?

I believe you do. And if so, don't you agree that it really is rather miraculous, this way in which something always 'turns up'? As though our love were so deep and strong that it had an actual physical power to enlarge our territories, to create something out of nothing.

Or is that being too fanciful? Maybe it is just a question of necessity being the mother of invention. Like those buses which transport the inhabitants of the Mediterranean down their sun-drenched valleys. Long after the bus is crammed to overflowing it continues to bounce from village to village, adding to its living cargo, receiving old women, hens, dusty soldiers, peasants, dogs, babies, and finding accommodation for all of them.

§ VI

At any rate the garden continued to grow. A new herbaceous border was dug on the other side of the centre wall, under the camellia tree. This meant sacrificing the only place where it was possible to sunbathe without anything on at all, but that could not be helped. Besides, while the bed was being dug, I had an idea for an odd sort of invention, that was like a mixture between a hip-bath and a cellophane umbrella, which could be wheeled on to the lawn as a shelter. It never came to anything, of course, but one day I may try it. (In return for a small fee, invitations will be issued for this occasion.)

There were also two tiny beds in two more corners, and a scooped-out patch that would do for primroses, and a great increase of vines and creepers. But it was the main herbaceous border that was the principal centre of excitement during this summer, for it was here that the roses were planted. And it was with the coming of the roses that the garden ceased to be a dream and became a reality.

Here is a list of the varieties that were contained in that first bunch. There was an *Angèle Pernet* of surpassing beauty. The catalogues describe this rose as, 'Inside of petals vivid orange-yellow, shaded reddish-apricot and outside golden yellow'. Irreverent people might think this sounds like a badly-poached egg, but we needn't bother about such brutes.

There was a *George Dickson*, one of the loveliest of the very dark roses. The darkest of all, of course, is the Irish rose *Night*, which really is like black velvet . . . or rather, like black velvet lying under a stained glass window, with the evening light drifting through a pane of smouldering crimson. But *Night* is too difficult for most of us. It shrivels in the sun and sulks in the shade. *George Dickson* stands up to the elements, sombre, stern, superb.

The finest specimen in the bunch was a *Madame Abel Chatenay* — an eternal rose, and to my mind the most exquisitely feminine of all. It reminds one of those roses that Boucher laid in the laps of his loveliest ladies, though it must be of a later period than that.

Frau Karl Druschki let me down, so there was no white rose. Personally I think that Frau Karl is going to the dogs. When I was a boy she was firm-breasted, upright, and of a dazzling purity. Of recent years she has been getting blowsy, fatigued and almost sallow. I bought her because I hoped she might have reformed. She hasn't.

But there was a *Lady Forteviot*, with a scent like a sun-warmed apricot, and a *Caroline Testout*, from whom Frau Karl should really take a lesson. For though Caroline is also a legendary lady, she has kept her complexion untarnished. Indeed it seems to flush more brightly every year, as though each summer whispered some secret which she recalled, in smiling memory, with every June.

Autumn, Katherine Pechtold, and *Etoile de Hollande* completed the list. Reading it over, it seems to add up to eight. There should have been twelve — no, eleven, in view of the misbehaviour of Frau Karl. But though there was not apparently a rose from every tree in that first bunch, they all flowered, freely enough, throughout the summer. And as we said before, with their flowering, the garden finally came to life.

CHAPTER XIV

THE ENCHANTED CORNER

IT should by now be glaringly apparent to all who have read so far that these adventures bear a striking resemblance to those of Louis XIV at Marly. In fact, my ideas about gardening are so like those of Le Roi Soleil that they can only be explained by the theory of reincarnation.

One of the things which I often said to myself, during that third summer, when the roses made the garden come to life, was, 'Well, it's such a tiny garden that I *can't* go on spending money on it like this, even if I try. Now that these borders have been made, and these beds and the fernery, I *can't* do much more. It's obviously impossible to have lakes, or waterfalls, or grottoes or rock-gardens. So really it doesn't matter spending rather a lot of money on the greenhouse' — (or whatever else might be the craze of the moment) — 'because there won't be the faintest opportunity to spend any more on anything at all'.

However, there was plenty of opportunity to spend a great deal more on a lot of things, as you will soon see.

But first let me explain about Louis XIV.

If you know your *Memoirs of Saint-Simon*, you will recollect that when Louis suddenly decided to build a château among the swamps of Marly, he chose this unpromising site simply because it *was* so unpromising. He knew his own weaknesses, and he did not want to be tempted as he had been tempted at Versailles. He did not want a place with much natural water because he knew that it would inflame his passion for fountains and aqueducts. He did not want much land, because he knew it would compel him to plant avenues (just as I had not dared to buy the rubbish-heap beyond the fence because I knew I should not be able to stop myself turning it into a swimming pool).

What happened? Listen to Saint-Simon:

> Gradually the place was enlarged; the terraces were dug away to give more space; the hill was almost entirely removed to give some sort of view; gardens were planned and made, and a park as well; waterworks and aqueducts were constructed; works of art, statues, and furniture were brought, and Marly became what we now see it, though much has been taken away since the King's death. Woods were planted, with full-grown trees brought from Compiègne; three-fourths of these died, and had to be replaced. (*That last sentence gives me the most poignant sympathy for Louis.*) The King was always making alterations, at great cost. I myself saw a large wood transformed within six weeks into a pond where people rode in gondolas. (*Which reminded me that Héloise had already archly suggested*

216

that I ought to flood the terrace, buy a canoe, and go for enormous 'twips' with her on the water.) This was scarcely accomplished when the lake was turned into a forest again, with such large trees that they kept out the light of day. The fountains and waterfalls were transported here and there a hundred times; carp-basins, decorated with gilt and beautiful paintings, were no sooner finished than they were taken elsewhere, with new decoration by the same painters. Such things happened again and again. One could safely say that, taking all this into consideration, with the expense of the prodigious device for raising water known as the Marly machine with its immense conduits, aqueducts and reservoirs, Versailles itself cost not so much as Marly. Such was the place that was originally covered with refuse, the haunt of frogs, toads, and snakes, chosen in the first instance because it was impossible to spend much money upon it. The King's haughty pride in overcoming natural difficulties is well exemplified at Marly, and neither the most serious war nor his conversion to religion was ever able to change him.[1]

All of which most regrettably applies, on a smaller scale, to my own activities at this period. But it was worth it.

---

[1] *Memoirs of Saint-Simon*, translated by Barret H. Clark.

§ 11

Now one of the things which it seemed quite certain that I should have to do without at Highways Close, was a rock-garden. There simply was not a square inch in which to build one. And you may take it from me that if I had decided there was not a square inch, nobody else would have been able to find a square inch either. For I had even toyed with the idea of having a miniature rock-garden on a trolley, which could be wheeled about and kept — well, somewhere. In a specially excavated cellar, presumably.

But somehow, the idea of building a cellar, creating a rock-garden on a trolley, and wheeling it out for an airing every day, as though it were an expensive baby, seemed a little too fantastic. Louis XIV might have done it, but he didn't have to pay income tax.

All the same, I hankered after that rock-garden. It seemed absurd not to have one. It was the very thing one *should* have, beyond all others. After all, circumstances compelled me to think in terms of Lilliput, and the whole charm of a rock-garden is Lilliputian. In the tiniest space one can have the greatest adventures. One can lean down, as Gulliver might have leaned, and walk in imagination through forests of flowers, scaling gigantic cliffs that are covered with the snows of the white saxifrage, looking long into deep blue pools of gentians. Whole heaths one can traverse when wearing Gulliver's shoes, and forget that they are only a few sprigs of heather. And the fragrance of a clump of dianthus — so tiny that all the flowers would hardly make a bouquet for a doll — seems in one's Gulliver mood as sweet as a field of lilies.

It was terrible, this rockless condition. And it grew worse with the passing of the snows. Now that I was once again a regular subscriber to the garden magazines, the advertisements of the rock-garden merchants seemed like a personal affront. Campanulas three inches high — that was one of the things which made me gnash my teeth. When they were planted, of course, they would shoot up like rockets, and cause Mrs. H. to congratulate me on the size of my hollyhocks, but that couldn't be helped. The advertiser *said* they would never be more than three inches high, and for some weeks, at least, one would have the pleasure of believing him. Belief is much more fruitful (and much saner) than doubt. Which is one of the secrets of a happy life, but we can't go into all that now.

§ III

Then, one day, I found it. The place for the rock-garden, I mean. I found it simply by walking up and down the terrace. Up and down, up and down, and then up again. And at the last up (which had brought me to the sunny corner by the entrance to the toolshed)

I suddenly stopped, looked down at the pavement, and said in a loud voice, 'Here!' Half the terrace must be torn up without a moment's delay. A rock-garden should appear in its place.

Why this vast expanse of terrace? Once again I asked myself, was I trying to emulate the House of Lords? What could any one man need with this interminable vista — nearly forty feet long — of arid stone?

An awful thought assailed me. If this end of the terrace were torn up, would the whole of the rest of the design of the garden be spoiled? I hurried to the window, held out my arm to cut out the right-hand part of the terrace, and tried to imagine it with nothing but rocks. I breathed a sigh of relief. The design remained. Indeed, it was actually enhanced.

Within half an hour, Mr. Peregrine was once more on the spot.

'I want you to take up all this side of the terrace, Mr. Peregrine.'

Mr. Peregrine blinked. '*All* this side?' he repeated.

'Yes, all of it. I'm going to make a rock-garden.'

Mr. Peregrine blinked again. I knew what he was about to say. He was about to say that he did-not-wish-to-deter-me-But. Which was precisely what he said.

The Buts were rather formidable. Apparently, all sorts of things went on underneath the terrace. Things whose existence one had not previously suspected, like drains, electric cables, gas pipes, and what not.

Dangerous things, explosive things, and things that smelt quite terrible.

It could not be helped. I told Mr. Peregrine that if necessary, all these things would have to be led away, conducted under the lawn, and joined up again beneath the rest of the terrace . . . (shades of Louis XIV!) . . . in some ingenious way which would surely occur to him after only the briefest consideration. That if necessary we would do without electric light, and live in a mellow glow of candle-light. That we would do without gas and cook in a chafing dish. That we would do — if the worst came to the worst — without drains, and go out to hotels. But we *had* to have the rock-garden, and so would he please tell his men to come round at the earliest opportunity.

His men came round that afternoon, and by the following evening nearly half the terrace had disappeared. The Buts proved to be much less formidable than we had feared. True, one of the workmen got an electric shock, but as he was rheumatic, it probably did him good. And for a short time there was an abominable smell. But that had nothing to do with either the drains or the gas. It just came from the earth itself, which was as foul and useless as any earth I had ever seen. It was almost a week before it was all carted away, and clean, sweet loam laid in its place.

§ I V

And now it all began again. The triangle business.
You may well sigh. You had every reason for thinking
that we had done with triangles for ever.

But just look at the photograph facing page 221, and
observe the space I had to deal with, and ask yourself
how you could do anything with such a hideous shape?
It was impossible. After all, making a garden is very like
painting a picture. And how could you paint any sort
of picture in such a frame? It was even worse than it
seems on the photograph.

The more I looked at it, the worse it seemed.

The practical difficulties were even greater than the
aesthetic. How, for example, was the toolshed to be
reached if a whole lot of rocks were piled in front of it?
One couldn't suddenly take a flying leap over it, particularly if one happened to be accompanied by a wheelbarrow. And what was to be done about the wall?
It would look ridiculous to pile rocks against a brick
wall. Yet, if one didn't do that, where was the rock-
garden to begin, or rather, to end?

However, at first, I let the practical difficulties go
hang and concentrated on the aesthetic. It is a fairly
safe rule in life that if a thing is beautiful it is also useful.
Ugliness is impracticable. Beauty is efficient. At any
rate, that's my own opinion, and though it does not seem
to be very widely held, I shall stick to it.

So I confined myself to trying to make a pleasing

design out of that corner — a frame that would be worthy of all the pretty things it was to shelter. But after prowling about for hours at a time, the only conclusion at which I had arrived was that somehow or other three bold lines must be drawn, as in the sketch below:

There *must* be three lines. The rhythm of the rest of the garden demanded it. Also, it was essential that they should be curved, in about the same degree as the path was curved.

But what was the line to *be*? In a moment of desperation I ordered a number of standard bays, six feet high. They might do the trick.

Unfortunately I was not there when they arrived, or

Joseph would have been spared the trouble of putting them in. They were horrible. They did not make a proper curve at all. And even had they done so, they would have been utterly out of keeping with the rocks, and they would have taken away a great deal of necessary nourishment from the plants themselves.

'I'm very sorry, Joseph. But they'll all have to come out.'

Joseph gave me a baleful glance, which I certainly deserved. The trees were removed. And there we were, *as* we were.

The days went by, and still nothing suggested itself, though I spent most of every morning and a large part of every afternoon, trying to get ideas. I even took to drink, and fell into the habit of having a glass of sherry to stimulate the imagination before emerging, taking up my position in front of that desolate corner, and waiting for ideas. They never came. Cavalier came, and rubbed himself against my legs. Rose came, and did the most distracting ballets for my benefit. Sometimes even Héloise came. But inspiration . . . never.

After several bottles of sherry had been consumed in this vain quest, I decided that the inspiration might flow more freely with the assistance of a paper and pencil. So I took to clipping sheets of foolscap on to volumes of Chopin études, taking out a chair, and sketching various possible designs. But they never came to anything. If the design looked all right, then I discovered that I'd got the angle of the wall all wrong.

Whenever I got that wall at the right angle, the design looked terrible.

I gave up the idea of sketching, and tried what could be done with my hands; half closing my eyes and making scooping gestures in the air to try to see if there was no way of extending the general 'rhythm' of the garden to this nasty little corner. This method sounds intolerably precious and affected. Perhaps it was. It certainly must have looked very strange, as though one were walking in one's sleep, or practising some exotic Indian dance.

It was during one of these moments, when I was stalking about like an amateur Svengali, that Héloise appeared.

'Practising?' she said brightly.

I rapidly withdrew my hands and glared at her. How *did* this woman get in? Gaskin had strict orders that I was out. Did she crawl through the cat-door, or what?

She advanced, regarded the corner, and sighed. Ecstatically. She was about to be glad about something.

'This is going to be . . . interesting,' she breathed.

It was too much. Interesting, indeed! Why should it be interesting to Héloise? Unbearable creature! I grabbed her by the arm, led her into the house, and compelled her to drink the last of the sherry. It had dregs in it, and made her choke. She looked rather attractive while doing so.

§ v

This has gone on long enough. It is simpler to publish another photograph and show you the ultimate solution.

I felt very unimaginative at having to resort to brick, but there was no other way out. I had to deal with such arrogant ugliness that arrogant methods were needed to combat it. The actual wall I built myself, brick by brick, with the assistance of a plasterer. It was lucky that there was the ceanothus in the background, because its branches, when stretched on to the new wall, seemed to make the whole thing blend together. I cannot imagine why I had not thought of curving the edge of the terrace before. It obviously had to be curved. In fact, as you will observe, *everything* had to be curved.

The design may not be perfect, but I do claim that it is among the best that were possible in the circumstances. And it bears out, by the way, my theory that beauty is utilitarian. The wall is in exactly the right place for the general design, and it happens to form a gap which is just wide enough for the wheelbarrow to pass through to the toolshed.

However, we are anticipating.

As soon as the wall was built, and the edge of the terrace curved, I found myself confronted by an unexpected hurdle of frightening proportions. Fortunately it proved to be the last, because if there had been any

more, I should have given up the whole thing as a bad job, and gone off to some place where life was less strenuous.

The hurdle was formed by the rocks themselves. When ordering them, I had thought, naturally enough, in terms of the usual weathered sandstone. This in due course arrived. It is pleasant to recall that I ordered far too much of it — so much, in fact, that the lorry broke down, and blocked up the drive for three hours, greatly incommoding a luncheon party at Mrs. Heckmond wyke's.

But any pleasure that might have been derived from this circumstance was dispelled when I went out and saw the rocks, piled up in a heap against the brick wall. They looked abominable. The grey, lichened stones fought so fiercely with the red brick that plainly it was a fight that could never be finished. It wasn't a mere question of colour. There is nothing intrinsically offensive about a grey stone against a brick wall. It was a question of . . . well, 'taste' sounds a silly, watery word, but it will have to do. The rocks were so stark, so suggestive of wind-swept moors, and the brick was so smooth, so obviously civilized, that it was as though I had asked Emily Brontë to meet Evelyn Waugh at tea. And if you can think of any worse predicament than that, you are welcome.

I turned to Joseph, who was sweating profusely, having done the lion's share of the rock transportation.

'I'm very sorry, Joseph,' I said. 'They'll all have to go back again.'

Joseph unbent himself, wiped the sweat off his forehead, and looked me straight in the eye.

'They aren't right,' I continued faintly, feeling very like a decadent slave-owner being fanned in the portico while women and children expired before him in the Virginian dust.

'What's wrong with 'em?'

'Everything,' I said.

Whereupon, I retreated. There was a look in Joseph's eye that I did not like. Those rocks were very heavy, and might cause considerable abrasions if skilfully directed. And Joseph, at that moment, would undoubtedly have been delighted to direct them at me. For which he is not to be blamed in the least.

Nevertheless, it was Joseph who eventually solved the problem. A few days later, when the last rock had been removed, and when things had calmed down, we had the whole thing out. I didn't tell him about asking Emily Brontë to meet Evelyn Waugh, but we went into the colour question pretty thoroughly, and Joseph, who has natural good taste, agreed that the grey rocks had looked 'pretty grim'.

'What about that Devonshire limestone?' he said suddenly. 'That with the red streak in it?'

'That's an idea.'

'You wouldn't have no clashing then.'

'I don't believe you would.'

I stared at Joseph. But I wasn't really seeing him. I was only thinking of the softer stone of that sweet and amiable county, the stone that seems to be eternally flushed with some of the southern sun that has drenched it through the centuries.

It was this stone that we obtained, after delays that seemed endless. And as soon as it arrived I knew that at long last it had found its appointed home.

§ VI

It is to be feared that after these purple passages, the photograph of the finished article (facing p. 226), may seem a little tame, particularly as it was taken, like all the photographs in this book, at the wrong time of the year. However, it should not seem so tame if you bear in mind that it is not a photograph of a suburban rockery at all, but a landscape of Lilliput.

There is far more in it than you can possibly guess. Far too much, you may say. Indeed when you look at the tiny space, and are told that *it contains nearly seventy varieties of plants*, you would be justified in thinking that it was absurdly overstocked. One energetic aubretia, or a couple of saxifrages that had been listening to Hitler and were consequently feeling the need of 'breathing space', would swamp the whole affair.

Maybe you are right. It will be impossible to reach a final conclusion for another two years, for the simple reason that the plants have not yet had time to spread to anything like their full capacity. But you are probably wrong, for two reasons.

Firstly, because every pocket is split into several self-contained sections, to a depth of nearly two feet, by slabs of slate. This means that even if the plants were allowed to get tangled above the surface (and they *won't* be allowed!) the roots would always be obliged to keep themselves to themselves. It is a simple matter to clip back an aubretia, or to rout out a clump of those little pink daisies which are always inclined to stray so far from home, but unless you divide the roots, in the manner indicated, you are only tinkering with the problem, and your last state will be worse than your first.

I used to think that the slate idea was my own invention. But one day, walking in the gardens of the Bagatelle in Paris, I saw that they used it there, which is yet another proof that great minds think alike.

The second reason why there is reason to hope that this little space is not overstocked lies in the nature of the plants themselves. They were chosen, after an exhaustive process of elimination, for their permanently Lilliputian qualities. It is putting rather a strain on your credulity, in view of that dreary photograph, to ask you to believe all this, but it really is true. And therefore, though you can't see them, I would recommend to your attention the following specimens, which you will find invaluable if, like most city gardeners, your space is drastically rationed.

Berberis Stenophylla. This is a complete berberis bush — (the common sort that is covered with small orange flowers in late April) — shrunk to a thirtieth of its normal size. The great thing about this, and about some of the other things that will be recommended, is that it is a miniature and not a midget. Do you get my meaning? No? Well, it can be explained by suggesting that the dwarf trees in Japanese gardens are midgets and that a *Narcissus cyclaminaeus* is a miniature. Those Japanese trees aren't natural — at least, not to me. They have the same uncanny quality that is to be found in the faces of dwarfs, a rather horrible blend of youth and age. The appearance of the dwarf is due to a deficient functioning of the thyroid gland, the appearance of the Japanese tree is due to various practices of constriction, starvation, and torture, inflicted on it in its infancy. So I am never happy about those Japanese trees. But I do feel very happy about my berberis, which was intended by Nature to grow that way.

Fuchsia Tom Thumb. Vital. No other word will suffice. Even if it means selling your star sapphires, you must have a Fuchsia Tom Thumb. Why? A, because it is a miniature and not a midget, like the berberis. B, because it is covered with idiotically small blossoms even in the most detestable weather. C, because in spite of the smallness of these blossoms, they are still poppable when in bud. There is a school of thought which contends that it is immoral to pop fuchsia buds, but like a lot of other immoral things I can't resist doing it. When one's friends pop them, it is odious, and one resolves never to ask them to the house again. But when one does it one-self, it is delicious. And one can always gain consolation from the thought that perhaps the buds like it. For after all, they are being saved a lot of hard work.

Paeony Tenuifolia. I can't write a long screed on why you should get this flower. It is enough to say that anybody who does not, is certifiable. For it produces paeonies the size of small scarlet buttons, surrounded by a most elegant ruff of emerald lace. It is, by the way, a great moral help to those who have not yet disciplined their minds to Lilliputian standards.

Aquilegia. Discolor and *Flabellata Nana Alba.* There are dozens of tiny aquilegias, completely neglected by other-wise sane people. The only reason for mentioning these two is because the *Discolor*, to quote the catalogue of the benefactor from whom I obtained mine, is 'one of the neatest and smallest of all. A Columbine with blue jackets and white skirts, two inches high'. These are entitled to rank as the beauty chorus of Lilliput. A line of them looks like a row of happy dancing girls.

The *Flabellata Nana Alba* (which somehow suggests a rather anaemic nursemaid), is of a different disposi-tion, but is none the less enchanting. It is, for Lilliput, enormous; it sometimes attains to the giant stature of a whole four inches. Never mind, for it is a dazzling white. Ask yourself what you are doing, sitting on the top of a lot of disgusting stocks and shares, when you might exchange them for such delights. Honestly, people with even *one* stock or share, who deny themselves the consolations of *Flabellata Nana Alba*, must be stark, staring mad. Which brings me to . . .

Lilium kikak. In contrast with what has gone before, this lily is of almost Brobdingnagian proportions, for an exceptionally tall specimen may sometimes shoot skywards to a height of nearly six inches, so that its tawny summit is almost lost in the clouds. However, if you imagine that these are the towers and steeples of Lilliput you need not be distressed. And very sturdy towers they are, that seem impervious to the wind and the rain and the soot. When you have scaled one of them, in imagination, you can look down at the other sections of the rock-garden, which in this mood suggest Housman's 'coloured countries', lying far below. You will see, over to the west, a lovely little coppice of flowers which gives you the strange feeling that the moonlight is shining on it. This is . . .

Phlox subulata, G. F. Wilson. It is an odd name for an enchanted wood, but we can't help that. Its flowers are star-shaped and drenched with this exquisite light, which hovers over them even in the glare of noon. I feel that this must be the meeting-place of all the various Lilliputian dwarfs, elves, goblins, and 'things that go bump in the night', though there is no positive evidence to this effect.

Leaving the magic phlox, we hurry away, and after a brisk walk of some twenty inches, we begin to sniff the air, which smells of honey, and to shade our eyes, which are dazzled by a golden light. As we turn round beneath a gaunt cliff, we see stretching before us a grove of *Genista Dalmatica.* The very sight of this makes you feel inclined to emulate Linnaeus, who, as every schoolboy knows, fell on his knees in rapture when he first sighted a hedge ablaze with English gorse. But it would be difficult, if not dangerous, to fall on your knees before the *Genista Dalmatica,* for it never attains to a height of more than three inches. As a sternly practical hint it should be mentioned that these exciting little bushes are very slow-growing indeed. In fact, mine appear to be completely stationary. So if you want to have a real grove of gorse, don't leave any spaces.

Well, we must turn our backs, with a sigh, on the fields of Lilliput . . . its valleys where the thrift waves like a rose-coloured sea, its precipices that foam with a white torrent of campanulas, its shady groves where the high pennants of the irises are hoisted. We must leave it, with all its bells and its blowing branches, its fragrance and its shifting lights. And we must go back to the great world that lies so many leagues away . . . to be precise, fifteen feet, at the end of the terrace.

CHAPTER XV

INVENTIONS

But, before we tell of the next advance (which will make Louis XIV's exploits at Marly seem very small beer indeed) we must do a certain amount of tidying up.

This involves, once more, retracing our steps. The pleasures of the rock-garden were so keen that they compelled us to hurry after them into the third spring, forgetting a number of minor adventures that had been occurring in the meantime. Therefore, if you please, consider that we are once more at the end of that summer when the advent of the roses made the garden a living thing.

Do you remember the little lead boxes that were placed behind the walls? In case you have forgotten, they came into being because the only bed available for paeonies was already filled by wallflowers. The idea of the wallflowers suggested the wall, and the idea of the wall suggested a box behind the wall, with the happiest results.

Well, if you look at the photograph facing page 194, you will see this intention carried to the extreme of elegance and, it must be added, of expense.

You will also see a memorial to the final skirmish in the Battle of the Dome.

You may recall that when the dome was at last completed, when the final girder was set and the final piece of glass laid in, I was assailed with faint feelings of guilt. It *did*, to be frank, look much larger than I had expected. In fact, I wished that it might have been possible to throw a cloth over it, in a casual manner, until people had got used to it. However, as the cloth would have had to be the size of several large billiard-tables, as it would certainly blow off, and as it would, in any case, make the thing more conspicuous than ever, I decided to beautify it in other ways.

It was on a golden Sunday evening in October that I fetched a pair of steps, clambered up the wall, and balanced myself on the ledge, to see what could be done about it. A golden Sunday evening of liquid sunlight and clean country air, through which the bell of the old church, high above, trembled with an unusual clarity. An evening when the smoke of the city seemed entirely banished; when the only smoke came from a pale column that hovered over a pile of burning leaves in a neighbouring garden.

Being Sunday, Mrs. H. was away, and so I could peer about to my heart's content. Mrs. H.'s fuchsias were doing very well indeed. That was saddening, though the gardener might be bribed to give me a cutting which, with my extra ration of sunlight, would certainly do better. Her red-hot pokers, too, were far too robust for

London. Embittering, that. But on the whole, the prospect was not too bad. A great many things seemed to be hanging on to life by the merest thread.

Filled with these charitable thoughts, I turned my attention to the space surrounding the dome. There was really quite a respectable area. It was formed, of course, by the irregular patch which, in the days when the garden had meant nothing to me, had so nearly been given away. I thanked heaven, not for the first time, that I had done nothing so foolish. To give Mrs. H. anything, regular or irregular, would have been more than any man could bear.

However, this was a mission of peace, and sweetness and light. Away with these thoughts! I saw that it would be the easiest thing in the world to fill the irregular patch with earth, and plant it with flowers which would delight the whole of the Close. And in a moment of abandon, I thought I would have a little leaden trough, in addition, all the way round the front. The result would probably look like the sort of 'toque' that one's mother wore in 1913, but there was no harm in that. For the first year the patch should be filled with white narcissus and white tulips, and the trough should be very formal with white hyacinths. If Mrs. H. didn't swoon with delight every time she looked at it, she would be no lady.

And then, as I was about to clamber down again, I thought of even another way by which coals of fire might be heaped on Mrs. H.'s head. I would write to her, tell her my suggestion, and ask if she approved. Perhaps she would prefer blue hyacinths? Or a mass of jonquils? Whatever she might say, I should be only too happy to oblige.

Feeling so inflated by these charitable sentiments that I was almost surprised that I did not float away on the evening air, like a large and amiable cloud, I turned. And immediately stumbled back with such force that if the dome had not been made of exceedingly thick glass, I should undoubtedly have fallen through.

For there, gazing up at me from the bottom of her garden wall, her face very pale and glistening in the half-light, was Mrs. H. How she had got there without being seen was a mystery. But then Mrs. H. had a genius for unexpected appearances.

For a moment which seemed an age we stared at one another. She was still wearing her beret, which implied that she had only that moment returned from the country. Also, she was extremely angry.

At last she spoke. She said one word. The one word in the English language which, when followed by a mark of interrogation, is calculated to arouse savage feelings in the most amiable breast. She said:

'Yes?'

Now there is very little to say in reply to that word, when it comes out of the blue, and when it is delivered in tones of ill-concealed hostility. If analysed, it betrays a great many meanings which have nothing whatever to do with a simple affirmation. It means, among other things,

'What are you doing here, you filth? How came it that such a loathsome creature could ever have been born? How is it that I am not at this moment strangling you to death?' All of these meanings, and many more, were implicit in Mrs. H.'s 'Yes?'

Well, one of the reasons why Mrs. H. was not at that moment strangling me to death, was because I was perched in a precarious position some ten feet above her head.

'I was just looking at the dome,' I said, with great feebleness.

'Oh?' Mrs. H. moistened her lips. 'Isn't it visible from your own garden?'

'This *is* my own garden,' I muttered. Which was true enough, for not an inch of me was projecting over the wall.

'Because,' continued Mrs. H., ignoring my remark, 'it's quite visible from mine. *Quite!*'

'Quite,' I echoed.

The idiotic conversation flagged. I longed to climb down, but felt that the attitudes it would be necessary to assume in doing so were far too grovelling to exhibit before Mrs..H.

'Your fuchsias,' I managed to gulp, 'seem to be doing exceedingly well.'

'Oh *no*.' Mrs. H. shook her head violently. 'They used to be a sight. A *mass*. That was in the days when they had sunlight. But now, of course . . .' She did not finish the sentence, but directed her eyes towards the

239

dome, implying that it had blocked out all trace of sunshine from their unhappy lives. As no shadow of the dome, at any time of day, came within ten feet of the fuchsias, this seemed to me an exaggerated statement, and I gently hinted as much.

And all that Mrs. H. said was . . . 'Yes?'

I have no idea how I eventually managed to descend from the dome. All I know is my knees were sore and my temper sorer. It was only after playing Delius's 'On First Hearing the Cuckoo in Spring' (which is enough to melt away every evil thought from the mind of man, enough, almost, to make one think tenderly even of Mrs. H.), that I sufficiently recovered myself to write her the little note which had been previously decided upon.

In it I observed, as politely as possible, that while the Dome Situation must be regarded as finally settled, as part of the history of Heathstead, I fully realized that its outlines might not appear, to some, as they appeared to me. The silver bubble which *I* saw, delicately encasing a host of exquisite things, might seem to other eyes a mere blot on the horizon. Let us therefore make the best of things. Let us surround it with flowers. Let us . . . I had a glass of sherry, and became quite rhapsodical. I called to Cavalier, and together we went round to Number 1, slid the note into Mrs. H.'s letter box, and tiptoed away.

On the following morning I received this reply:

'Mrs. Heckmondwyke presents her compliments to Mr. Beverley Nichols, and regrets that his letter is incomprehensible to her. Mr. Beverley Nichols has already given such marked and, she may add, outstanding proof of his independent aesthetic tastes, that she feels that any decorative suggestions on her part would be regarded (as they have apparently been regarded in the past), as an unwarranted intrusion.

'In this case Mrs. Heckmondwyke can only assume that Mr. Beverley Nichols has forwarded his letter to the wrong address. Acting upon this assumption, she has redirected it to Mr. and Mrs. Howard, who she is sure will appreciate it as it deserves.'

Upon receipt of this letter, I made a solemn vow to fill every available inch of earth around the dome with leeks, nettles and poison ivy. Needless to say, the vow was broken. White hyacinths, white tulips, and white narcissi it was. And in the summer, pink ivy-geraniums. If you will look again at the very inadequate photograph (facing page 94) of the result, you may perhaps agree that Mrs. H. had not much to complain about.

§11

The next invention comes partly from New York and partly from Paris.

You may remember that earlier in our chronicle we referred to the cat problem, which sooner or later presents itself to every city gardener. A full life, it will generally be agreed, demands both a garden and a cat, but sometimes (particularly during planting out) life can be almost too full, if your cats are as keen on gardening as mine. Each plant has to be inspected, and if possible rolled upon. And the places where you desire to dig holes are invariably the places which the cat chooses for a long, deep sleep.

The problem therefore resolves itself into two parts: how to keep the cats off the beds, and how to do it without offending them. Put personally, how was I to enjoy the garden and at the same time to continue to enjoy the company of Rose and Cavalier?

Well, it was during my last visit to New York that one part of this problem was solved. I had been wandering about in Central Park, and had paid my usual visit to a certain secret spot in that pleasaunce where, if you stand on one leg, turn the head sharply to the left and shut one eye, you can see only the extreme top corner of the Ritz Tower, thereby gaining a feeling that you are, by comparison, in the depths of the country. Wild horses would not drag from me the position of this rural retreat. But if you do find it, please have your excuse ready for the cops. If they see you in this attitude they may think it odd. The best thing to do is to say that you are studying Yogi.

Returning to the city, I strolled down the streets, and suddenly came to a gardening shop. This made me feel very homesick, for it would soon be spring, and the shop was full of people asking questions about how many inches things ought to be planted, and would so-and-so come up earlier if you put it in six weeks before the instructions on the packet. Whenever I am in a garden shop I feel like jumping on the counter and making a speech, because people oughtn't to be allowed to buy such beautiful, precious things as seeds and bulbs if they are only going to maltreat them. However, I didn't make a speech on this occasion, because there was something on a tray which demanded instant inspection.

The something was called Catnip (I am *not* being paid to advertise it, though they ought to give me a director-ship). It was made up in little green tubes. It said on the outside that if you undid the capsule and hung the tube near a bed of flowers, it made such a horrible smell that no cat or dog would come near it. You couldn't smell it yourself. It was the cat's funeral.

Well, I bought a great deal of this preparation, and almost the first thing I did after reaching home was to try it out. And it worked! It worked almost too well. For when I undid the first tube, in the presence of Rose, I allowed him to sniff it. The expression on his face indicated not only nausea for the Catnip, but unutter-able disdain for myself for having taken advantage of his trustful nature. It was days before he forgave me.

But in the meanwhile, the Catnip (which lasts for six months) was defending the garden as it had never previously been defended. Stray cats would arrive, jump down from the wall, and walk with leisurely footsteps to the herbaceous border. They would step on to the border, for purposes which need not be divulged in detail. Then, just as they were about to begin, a look of horror would come over their faces. They seemed to be saying, 'What *is* it? Who *could* be responsible for such a deplorable aroma?' Whatever they were saying, they always beat a hasty retreat.

The smell, be it added, is only local. Rose and Cavalier still frisk up and down the path, do ballets on the lawn, and tear about in the shrubbery outside the front door. But the beds they leave alone. They gaze at the flowers from a respectful distance.

The Paris end of this invention can be very shortly described. It sometimes happens that you don't want cats even on the lawn. On such occasions it really is necessary that you should provide them with a substitute for grass, which is a sort of medicine for them. Well, do you know about *herbe pour chats*? I didn't, till quite recently. It is simply a specially succulent form of grass which you buy in Paris. I first encountered it when wandering down one of the quais — rows and rows of little pots, standing in line, each filled with bright green grass. 'Who eats the green grass?' I inquired. 'It is the cat of your father who eats the green grass', responded the lady, or words to that effect. So I bought some pots to the great delight of Rose and Cavalier. And you might do the same. You fill yourself with salads, under the vain delusion that you would look even more awful if you didn't; you are miserable if you don't get enough 'roughage' and vitamins and all that nonsense; but you never think that the poor cat might be worrying about its figure too. So please do something about it.

§ I I I

Invention number three brings us back into the domain of aesthetics.

It brings us into the garden by night.

Why do so many people seem to think that the moment the light is faded, the garden is dead? It is very difficult to understand. Sometimes in summer, by the full moon, they venture out to sniff a rose or two, and maybe to kiss somebody who would much prefer to be kissed comfortably on a full-sized sofa. But that is as far as they get.

They do not realize, for example, the almost unbelievable beauty, after dark, of *white* flowers. Admittedly it's not easy to have much white in a city garden, particularly if your space is limited. But for those who have large suburban gardens, or even for those who have only a border or two, and a bed here and there, and a very narrow path, there are many white nights of enchantment waiting round the corner, if only they would turn it.

It was, indeed, in a suburban garden that I was shown one of the loveliest white borders that I have ever encountered. I can see it, savour it, to this day. There were tobacco flowers, of a fragrance so poignant that it seemed to float on the air like a living spirit. Border pinks, mingling their own simpler scent. A branch of syringa, phosphorescent in the half-light. Foxgloves like tall tapers, standing in the dusk that was cast by a guelder-rose, in whose depths the petalled snows still lingered. Silver from the centaurea that flanked the deserted pavement, ivory from the rose that climbed the wall, and white again, pure and dazzling, from the lilies, that stood aloof, as though this exquisite procession were for their eyes alone.

For me and for most of us there can be nothing like that. But I have my own white border too, and very comforting it is to bend over it, after the heat and the clamour of the city. Here are stocks, rich and creamy, and the white stars of violas. In their season come the parchment-coloured irises of Japan, and the thickly-crowded blossoms of sweet william. Next year, perhaps, there will be a phlox or two, some white snapdragons, and some of the silver-leaved centaurea, if it can bear the city's murk.

We have been led, by these distant snows, far from the path on which our feet were set. That path is the same little curved path down which we have been walking all the time.

If you were to walk down it late at night, you would suddenly see shining before you, the head of an old faun, which hangs on the centre wall. You would probably jump, because you would not have noticed me switching on the light. But after that you would certainly agree that he is rather a nice old thing. He may look dissipated, but at least he is decorative.

You cannot see the faun in the picture, because he did

not arrive till after the photograph was taken. He would not have come out very well in any case, because his complexion is terra-cotta, faded by centuries of Italian sunshine, and during the day he blends into the brick. It is at night that he comes alive. For after he was placed there Mr. Peregrine was persuaded to lay a wire under the grass to the herbaceous border, and to put in an electric light flush with the earth. It is protected by a small glass box, and is practically invisible.

When the light is switched on, the faun seems to blink, and smile and sparkle. And though it is only his face that is lit, he casts a glow over all the flowers that may be blooming.

§ I V

'Vulgar,' you may snort. 'Very vulgar indeed.'

Or if you don't snort it, somebody else will. They really will. People are like that.

Why?

Why is floodlighting vulgar?

Why should it be considered any more vulgar to light a garden than to light a room? If I had a great deal of money and a cherry orchard, I should most certainly arrange for the orchard to be gaily and cunningly illuminated at night. It could be so planned that the thin green wires would be unseen during the day, and if the bulbs were very tiny they could be concealed among the foliage and the blossom. Think of walking down with a friend on a dark night, and then pressing a button and seeing a whole sea of blossom leap into sight, with countless little silver stars sparkling through it!

If that is vulgar, then the Statue of Liberty is vulgar. Or the candle-lit procession that wends its way, year by year, up the sacred slopes of Mount Lykabbetus. Or a lighthouse in an Atlantic storm. Or the sparks from the engine that speeds you from Vienna to Semmering . . . those unforgettable, rose-coloured sparks that glitter over the pine trees like magic dust. Or any fire that man has lit, since time's beginning, for his comfort, or his safety, or his delight.

Anyway, to come down to earth, you will have gathered by now that I like light in a dark garden even more than in a dark room. And one of the ways by which it was obtained in mine, was from the dome.

Not content with the light inside, I put very small lights *outside* (heavily frosted). When they were turned on, the dome really *did* look like a silver bubble floating in space, and all the flowers in the garden woke up.

Worst of all, for those who think all this so terribly vulgar, I added one or two lights of a deep indigo blue, so that the dome could be turned, according to one's fancy, into a jewel . . . fantastic, incredible, absurd . . . any adjective you like, provided that you always couple it with the word 'Beautiful'.

§ v

It seems almost superfluous to tell you that this innovation brought me into sharp conflict with Mrs. H. You must have been expecting it, just as I did. After a week or so had gone by, I was astonished that the bombshell had not yet fallen. The dome was always illuminated for at least a few minutes between the hours of six and seven, and there had been a cocktail party when it had been in full blaze from half-past five till nearly nine. Why had she not protested?

No doubt it was because she was awaiting a suitable opportunity — a really gross violation of her rights. Chance favoured her. I happened to come home one night very late with a friend, and I could not resist the temptation of turning on the lights (including the blues) just to show off. Unfortunately, having turned them on, I drew the curtains and quite forgot to turn them off again. When Gaskin woke me in the morning, he not only told me that the lights had been left on, but added — as if there were a sinister connection between the two events — that Mrs. Heckmondwyke had telephoned to say that she would be obliged if I could spare her a few moments after breakfast.

Well, there *was* a sinister connection. Mrs. H., through my oversight, had been presented with a superb martyr's role, and she was determined to extract every ounce of sympathy out of it.

When she was shown into my sitting-room, she sank into a chair, registering exhaustion.

'Forgive me,' she murmured, 'very tired.' She drew her hand over her eyes. 'Not a very good night.'

I made sounds of commiseration. Mrs. H. drew her hands away from her eyes, lifted her head, and peered, heavy-lidded, out of the window. 'Ah!' she breathed, 'I see it's off.'

'Off, Mrs. H.?' I inquired, knowing full well what she meant.

'The dome,' she explained — (and really, by now, she was beginning to pronounce it as though it were spelt 'doom') — 'I wondered if it was to be . . . perpetual.'

'Perpetual?' (They were the only safe retorts, these idiotic echoes.)

'I wondered,' and her voice gained a certain resonance in spite of her determination to be feeble and oppressed, 'if we were to have it by day as well as by night.' She paused, achieved a smile. 'Yes?'

'Certainly not, Mrs. H., if you are referring to the light in the greenhouse' (I tried to say 'Yes?' but could not manage it). 'Certainly not. It was an . . .'

'I know,' she interrupted, 'that I have absolutely no right to complain. None. As far as the legal situation is concerned' — (so she'd been to the lawyers *again*!) — 'as far as that goes, I gather that you can have a nightly display of rockets shooting from all sides of the dome' (pronounced, quite definitely, doom).

'It would be rather expensive, Mrs. H.'

She ignored me. 'You can have flood-lighting sixty times as powerful as it is at present, and you could make it revolve, into the bargain.'

'That's an idea,' I observed with enthusiasm.

'Yes?' Oh, the sweetness of that smile! 'Perhaps we may expect something of the sort. Yes?'

This was becoming much too strained.

'Really,' I began again. 'You have no cause to worry. It was an . . .'

She held up her hand. 'No cause?' she inquired, oh, so gently. 'Don't you think I have a *little* cause? To be asked to sleep in a blaze of light?'

'Oh, surely, Mrs. H. . . .'

'Of red, white and blue lights, rather. Doesn't that give me a little cause? Up to now I have always been used to sleeping in the dark. Old-fashioned of me, but . . .'

'I have tried to explain that it was . . .'

'I am not accustomed to sleeping in Piccadilly Circus. No.' She shook her head vigorously.

'It would be a most old-fashioned thing to do,' I suggested. 'But it was an *accident*, Mrs. H. It won't happen again.'

'No?'

'And if by a hundredth chance it should, you have only to draw your curtains and any slight glow which might be visible through your window . . .'

'I'm afraid I should be asphyxiated,' she sighed, 'if I drew the curtains. Besides, somehow I like to think that in my own house I still have the right to refrain from drawing the curtains if I wish.' She smiled heroically, and looked at me, her head on one side. 'Or have I? It would be interesting to know. These laws! An Englishman's home . . .'

She rose to go. At the door she paused. 'There's just one other thing,' she said. 'Your . . . your gargoyle.'

I did not hear her rightly. Her martyr-complex was causing her to mutter.

'I'm what, Mrs. H.?'

'Your little . . . ahem . . . gargoyle.'

'Oh, the faun?'

'Is it — I mean, *must* it be illuminated too? Quite so suddenly?'

'Well, I don't see how . . .'

'You see — forgive me, I know it's none of my business — but my little niece is coming to stay with me next week.'

'Yes?' I remembered the little niece. A great strapping girl of fourteen who, according to Gaskin, had given the butcher-boy a look which could 'Only Mean One Thing'.

'Highly-strung,' said Mrs. H.

Well, that was one way of putting it.

'At a critical age,' she continued.

That certainly seemed to be true.

'I feel that if she were to look out of the window, and see illuminated gargoyles flashing all over the garden in the middle of the night, she might perhaps be made a little restless. What do you think?'

'Does she spend much time at night looking out of the window?'

'That is hardly the point, is it?'

'It seems to be relevant.'

'It would be nice to think my guests *might* be allowed to look out, if they wished.'

'Oh, very well, Mrs. H. If you think she'd be scared I certainly won't turn it on at all.'

'*Please!*' She looked most distressed. 'I had no intention of asking you to make such a sacrifice.'

'It's no sacrifice.'

'I'm sure it would be. I know how necessary these constant excitements are for some people. I myself am content with a garden. I have *no* wish to live in the centre of a circus. None at all. But then, as you know, I am very old-fashi . . .'

I could not bear any more of it. 'Then I will be old-fashioned too, Mrs. H. Just for once.'

More by physical force than by persuasion, I led her from the room, still protesting, and guided her through the front door.

We said good-bye. And the expression on both our faces, as we did so, was very old-fashioned indeed.

CHAPTER XVI

THE DESERT BLOSSOMS

AT this point in our floral pilgrimage the scene shifts sharply to Woolworth's.

It is now fashionable to go to Woolworth's. For those who have been going there since the age of ten, it is a little too fashionable. There is something rather 'hot-making' (to use a good old English expression) about some of the sights one sees there nowadays. One has gone there oneself on quite legitimate business, to buy a lampshade or some cocktail glasses or some woollen gloves or some of the astonishing range of infernal machines they provide for the kitchen. While one is humbly clutching this sort of thing in a paper parcel, one is slapped on the back by a glittering creature, smelling of everything that Schiaparelli forgot to think of, and screaming, 'My *dear*! Look! *Sixpence!*' She holds out a bright red brooch. 'It's *not* to be believed, do you think? And my dear . . .' (here she fumbles in her What-not, by Cartier, and produces a couple of lipsticks). 'Three-pence *each*!' she screams. 'I shall go *mad*. It's too much heaven, isn't it?' The passers-by regard her curiously. 'I've just ordered a *pound's* worth of the maddest opal bracelets,' she affirms. 'One can hang them up in the garden to frighten away the *birds*. Darling . . . I couldn't be more delighted. Let's lunch, some time, shall we? Off this delicious Woolworth china, and then we can *break* it into a *thousand* pieces.'

She oozes away. More and more curiously the customers regard her.

Of such women are revolutions made. And rightly.

To resume, as they say at board meetings. On one of my strictly utilitarian visits to Woolworth's (sixpenny-worth of grape hyacinths it was this time) I chanced to see at the jewellery counter a quantity of bright blue brooches, that looked as if they were made from butter-flies' wings. Normally, I am not a devotee of such adorn-ments. I would prefer that the butterflies were allowed to flutter about undisturbed, in their native land. Their lives are short enough, without making them any shorter. Besides, the brooches, when affixed to bosoms, are definitely worrying. The bosoms heave, and so do the brooches. It is all very unrestful, and not to be en-couraged.

But as there was no bosom waiting for me to adorn it, and as the young lady behind the counter told me that the brooches weren't made from real butterflies' wings at all ('though you couldn't possibly tell the difference, could you?') . . . it was another matter. They were just a lot of pleasantly gaudy symbols. And I thought how attractive a flight of them would look against the pink walls of the loggia.

So I bought forty of the butterfly brooches, at sixpence

each. An embarrassing thing to do, when you come to think of it.

While waiting for the brooches to be done up, I wandered along to another counter, and saw that Woolworth's had become cactus-conscious. What next? I looked at them without much interest. Most of them were rather dull varieties of *mammillaria*, but one or two had small flowers just about to come out on the tops of their heads. There was something rather appealing about that. Partly to see what colour the flowers would be when they came out, and partly because — well, partly because they were only sixpence each — I bought half a dozen.

And that was another step on the road to ruin.

§ 11

The butterflies were a *succès fou*. The last word in affectation, as had been the intention. They flew across the pink walls like one of the more curious fancies in the spiritual life of Barbey d'Aurevilly. Little by little they changed the whole décor of the loggia. A few days later I found myself back at Woolworth's buying a set of fantastic glass dishes, peacock green in colour. A fortnight after that, Mr. Peregrine was summoned to paint the ceiling a brilliant blue. I tried to get some gold stars to stick on it, but nobody seemed to have any. So I contented myself with hanging from the ceiling an old

Venetian lamp, star-shaped and newly gilded. On the floor was laid linoleum faked to look like red marble.

It sounds torture. It sounds cruelty to animals. But it was very gay and idiotic.

All these changes brought me constantly into the loggia. One day, when I was sitting there, gazing in an ecstasy of idleness at the butterflies and the plates and all the other monstrosities, it struck me that this was really one of the sunniest corners of the garden. It also struck me — and here I rose abruptly to my feet, staggered by the significance of the discovery — that here was yet another place where things could be grown! If the roof were stripped off, and changed for glass, and if big glass doors were set in the open entrance, it would give me quite a sizeable greenhouse. Moreover, it would not be so very expensive — (my mind, I confess, was already running on domes) — because the loggia was connected to the dining-room, and one would only need to extend the hot-water pipes through the wall.

The more I thought of it, the more attractive it seemed. Only one thing worried me. The butterflies would have to go. As soon as one began to do any watering, their wings would drop off. Also, I reflected sadly, the pink walls would get very spotty. And the linoleum would be rotten after a single winter. In fact, the whole thing would look like a rococo edition of that novel which our grandmothers made into a best-seller — *The House on the Marsh*.

Still . . . *tout lasse, tout casse, tout passe* . . . all, that is to say, except green things that are growing, and even they must die one day. Far better to have a greenhouse than to sit brooding over a lot of butterflies. This was a time for great and heroic decisions. I telephoned to Mr. Peregrine, hardly daring to tell him that his beautiful blue ceiling would have to come down almost before the paint was dry on it, in order to give place to another dome.

Just as I was about to lift the receiver, I observed that one of the flowers on the cacti (which were sitting on a sunny ledge by my desk) had come out. It was such an unusual, smouldering shade of orange that I took it up to look at it. It was delightful. I reached for a magnifying glass. But really . . . an enchanting object. Like one of those elaborate Victorian brooches, with a topaz in the middle and a great deal of golden filigree surrounding it.

And to think that this bizarre and complicated blossom had produced itself from such a barren stick of a thing, which had been given no water for over a month!

No water! I looked over my shoulder towards the loggia. No water! Cacti could flourish out there, side by side with butterflies, linoleum, pink walls and every thing else! No water! Oh, most certainly, the loggia must become a cactus house. If ever the moving finger was writing its ordinances for my instruction, it was at this moment.

I replaced the cactus on its shelf, wondering if I was making a fool of myself.

After all, I knew nothing about cacti. And until this

question of dryness had arisen, it must be admitted that I had the prejudices against them which — in all probability — you share yourself. It wasn't only a question of saying, 'Nasty prickly things!', and leaving it at that. They did seem to be symbolic of a host of things which I actively disliked.

Bogus interior decorators, for example. There was a period in New York—mercifully it seems to be already labelled with the word *jadis* — when all the interior decorators went mad about cacti. They rushed round the city, in pink and blue cars, hugging *Mesembryanthema* to their camel-hair coats as if they got a real kick out of it, which perhaps they did. And then they shot up in elevators to rich apartments, kissed the old harridans to whom they happened to be appointed at the moment, and detached themselves — very reluctantly — from the *Mesembryanthemum*, which was given a place of honour in front of a bright red screen entirely covered with orange reindeer.

That, you will agree, is a true description not only of an epoch in the history of the cactus, but of an epoch in the history of America.

Well, that was one of my reasons for disliking cacti. Another reason was because once, owing to an over-intimate association with some *Neo-mammillaria*, in the Exotic Gardens at Monte Carlo, I had been unable to sit down for a week. If that sounds peculiar, it is not my fault.

So was it not madness to embark on such a large adventure with so small a reason? Better toss up for it.

If it came down heads — cacti; if it came down tails —
no cacti. It came down tails. Out of sheer annoyance
with the penny's perversity, I decided to have them.

Within a few hours, Mr. Peregrine was once more
sighing and shaking his head in the loggia. It was all
going to be very unpractical, very illegal and very
expensive, though it may not look it in the photograph.
Even the smallest dome would have to be specially made,
and the complexity of fitting glass round the little pillar
made the construction of the Pyramids seem child's play.
However, I was not to be deterred. For in the meantime,
I had snooped out and bought a book on Cacti, and the
things it revealed were of a nature to make one's blood
run high with anticipation.

§ I I I

At this point, presumably, there should be a short
'How-To-Begin' section, bristling with facts as prolific
and as pointed as the spines on a *Gymnocalycium Schicken-
dantzii*. (I didn't have to look that one up. I remembered
it on the same theory of nomenclature as we employed
in the case of the ferns. Only this one is too silly to put
into print.)

However, that sort of thing is done far better by the
professionals. There are a number of books on cactus-
growing which give you most of the main facts you ought
to know, though it is wisest to stick to *one* book, once you
have bought it, because writers on cacti seem to dislike

each other very much, and waste a lot of time in being madly sarcastic at each other's expense.

Besides, my own way of beginning, which is not recommended by any of the experts, seems as good as any other. Summing it up, it fell into four stages, which you might care to remember, in case you feel inclined to copy them. Here they are:

A   Go to Woolworth's, and buy a dozen.

B   Buy a book, and bore yourself by learning their abominable names.

C   Go to the nearest Botanical Gardens, enter the Cactus House, take off your overcoat, and wander round gaping for at least an hour, making notes of the things that please you. I went, as usual, to Kew, and disgraced myself by snorting with laughter at a large number of plants that could not answer back.

D   Order a small collection from a cactus specialist, according to the size of your purse. For a couple of pounds you can buy more than enough to keep you busy for years. It is necessary to remember that in ordering you should describe the exact nature of the accommodation you can provide, in terms of heat, light, attention, etc.

It is *no* good, at the beginning, trying to make a collection from seeds. By all means get a packet of seeds also, if only for the joy of seeing the first one come up (it looks like a baby's tooth). But don't kid yourself that you will be clever enough or lucky enough to grow a whole collection by these methods.

Instead, therefore, of writing a section on 'How To Begin', it will be more profitable, and more amusing, to write a section on '*Why* To Begin'. I want you to be 'sold' on cacti, to realize the great number of adventures that they will offer you ... some grotesque, some educational, and many of them beautiful.

The first reason why you should begin to collect cacti is, unexpectedly enough, for their *colour*.

Do you remember the colours we discovered hiding in the ferns — the blues, the saffrons, the golds and the silvers? Most people think of ferns as a monotonous assembly of greens. We proved that opinion to be a libel. In the same way, we can now give the lie to the people who think that cacti are mostly grey, or drab, or stony. You will find, as soon as you begin, that a wide range of new and marvellous colours will be at your disposal. If you are not as thrilled as a child with a new paint-box, you must be an awful person to have about the house.

For example, if you could walk out into the 'loggia' at this moment, you would see a plant which is as beautiful as any orchid (and nothing like as expensive). Since you *must* order it in your first collection, here is its name ...

Echeveria metallica. This is not, strictly speaking, a cactus at all, but it is one of the many succulents which grow in the same localities, demand the same treatment, and have the same habits.

It is impossible to describe the colour of this plant. It is more a question of light than of colour. There are ten leaves, grouped rather in the shape of a tulip, and each leaf is covered with a bloom that is as thick as the bloom on a bunch of hothouse grapes. The colour, too, is grape-like, except at the edges . . . and these are tinted with a rose so radiant that the plant always seems to be standing in the light of dawn. Indeed, I have christened my own plant 'shepherd's warning'. This isn't a matter of 'imagination'. It is a matter of fact. A very wonderful fact, too, as though it had some strange power to summon the early desert sunshine into the darkness of the city.

There are a number of other succulents in the *Echeveria* group which have this same queer quality of light. One is the *Echeveria perelegans*, which seems to be always steeped in moonlight, just as the *metallica* is always facing the dawn.

The colours that you will find in cacti are colours to be found nowhere else in the world, not even in the windows of Saks, Fifth Avenue, when the new spring hats are on view. It is as though Nature kept a special part of her palette reserved for them, and whenever she happened to mix anything extra striking or bizarre, said to herself, 'Nobody but a cactus could wear *that*'.

Consider the *Mammillaria Karwinskiana*. Not only does it produce a quantity of tiny flowers of so brilliant a yellow that they almost hurt the eyes, but these flowers are borne on stems (which are really pods) painted a fierce magenta. The effect is like something that we have not seen since the days of Bakst.

And what about the *Echinocactus* group? The fascination of these is partly due to their colour and partly due to the fact that the flowers seem to be made of the finest silk. There are all sorts of materials in Nature, from the velvet of the pansy to the parchment of the magnolia. But for *silks*, pure, glistening, of the highest quality, you must go to the cactus.

Some of these silks are patterned in a manner which recalls the most garish days of the French Regency. I will leave you to make your own experiments, and will only mention one, the *Echinocactus pampeanus*. It is a Chinese imperial yellow with a bright purple stripe, and if any woman wore it at the Ritz she would be asking for the worst.

§ I V

Well, that is one reason why you ought not to continue to live without cacti. For though you may not go off the deep end about it, you know quite well that there is not nearly enough colour in your life, and that you would be very much better if your days were shot through with a few more streaks of purple and orange. Cacti recall the times which Browning celebrated:

When reds were reds and greens were greens.

In the present era of browns and blacks it would therefore seem as though cacti had a very important part to play.

The next reason for becoming a cactus enthusiast is somewhat difficult to put into words. Strictly speaking, it is not a horticultural reason at all. Perhaps it would be best to sum it up under the general heading of 'Interest', like those Nature films which cover all subjects from the mating habits of the red spider to the summer sports of the Four Hundred. (It is not always easy, by the way, to know which of these two films one is watching, particularly if one has come in late, and has not had the opportunity of reading the title.)

'Interest' is rather a mild word for the emotions that you will feel when you begin to know your cacti really well. Look! There is one which seems to be producing a baby on the top of its head. Of all the crazy things! And here is one that has a whole troop of babies round its feet. If I break one off, will it grow? Yes, it will! And here is one with a wig, and one with a bright green flower. Who thinks these things up? And here is one . . . but *where* is it? It seems to have disappeared. No, here it is again. Hiding itself among all those pebbles.

Ah . . . you have discovered one of the most 'interesting' of all. It belongs to a group for which we might coin a name. We will call it . . .

The Camouflage Group. This is not the proper name, but let's use it to describe all those ingenious little succulents which imitate their surroundings. They will give you an endless amount of fun.

Camouflage in Nature is an alluring subject of study. True, it is not always all that it is made out to be. The only time I ever saw a chameleon it was sitting on a patch of bright red earth looking as green as a cabbage. The longer it sat, the greener it became. Perhaps it was colour-blind. Or maybe it was of a revolutionary disposition. Anyway, it lamentably failed to do its stuff. If you had put it on a patchwork quilt it would not have exploded; it would have assumed the tartan of the Macintoshes.

However, cacti and succulents are more obliging. Particularly the *Lithops*.

Please try to remember the name of the *Lithop* family. (All you need do is to think of an intoxicated bell-boy, though it is to be hoped that you will keep your thoughts decently controlled.) Their talent for camouflage is not the only reason why they should endear themselves to you. For instance, they produce delicate and idiotic little flowers in the middle of their stomachs; they look as if they had gone to a fancy dress ball and accidentally stuck a miniature marigold in their navels. But the flowering period, alas, is brief and erratic. For the rest of the year they amuse themselves by impersonations. There is hardly a pebble on the beach which they and their friends[1] will not imitate to perfection.

Which reminds me. If you want to get the full enjoyment out of the Swiss Family *Lithop* you must remove

[1] Such as the *Conophytum Leopoldii* and the *Argyroderma Tesichlare*. I put these names down here because they are really too fatiguing to be allowed to hold up the story.

them from their pots (in early May, a week after watering them) and transplant them into your main bed of
prepared earth. After you have done this, you must take
a train to Brighton, or Atlantic City, according to taste.
And there you must wander up and down the beach,
filling your pockets with scores of tiny pebbles of all
shapes and sizes. There is no law against this as yet, on
either side of the ocean. Then, when you come home,
you must spread the pebbles round the *Lithops* and their
friends, and before you have half finished, you won't be
able to tell them apart.

Some of the writers on cacti will tell you, in voices
trembling with rage, that this is a wicked practice — to
quote one of them, 'You may easily be misled into
thinking the soil underneath is dry, whereas it may be
sodden'. But surely you must be pretty sodden yourself
if you can be misled as easily as that? It would not seem
beyond the powers of human ingenuity, when in doubt,
to lift up a pebble, to apply the forefinger of the right
hand to the soil, and then . . . having closed the eyes and
concentrated for a few minutes . . . to decide whether it
was wet or dry. However, here we are, like all the other
cactus writers, becoming acidulous. And there are too
many delightful things awaiting our attention for us to
lose our tempers over such trifles.

§ v

The last reason why you should become a cactus fan — (there are hundreds of others, but we can't go on for ever) — is in order that you may have a good laugh. Just as Nature seems to have chosen them as the most suitable mannequins for her brightest colours, so she seems to have reserved them for the honour of interpreting her most boisterous fancies.

Which brings me to the *Cephalocereus senilis*. Whatever else you may choose to deny yourself, you must not deny yourself this.

I hate favouritism towards flowers almost as much as favouritism towards animals. On the happy occasions when I am surrounded by large quantities of dogs or cats, I feel uneasy if any one of them goes unpatted or unstroked. And though the screams of the hard-boiled school of critics are certain to rend the air after this confession, it is the same with flowers. When making a bunch of mixed flowers from a border, I have sometimes picked one which I don't really want at all, in case it should feel neglected. A habit which no doubt carries sensitivity to the pitch of sickliness. But the world wouldn't be much worse off in these days if a few people *were* a little more sensitive.

However, in spite of these sentiments, and in spite of the possibility that cacti may be able to read, and may therefore be offended by the words that follow, it must be confessed that of all my collection I feel most tenderly towards the *Cephalocereus senilis*. The name, of course, is appalling. It makes you so tired that you want to go upstairs and lie down. In order to prevent you from doing that, we will hasten to give it another name, which really fits it much better. We will call it . . .

The Matinée Woman. Do you ever go to matinées? Yes? Well, can you tell me a single occasion when you have gone to a matinée and failed to sit behind an elderly lady, with untidy grey hair? No, you can't. Nobody has ever been to a matinée and sat behind anything else. It can't be done.

I am very fond of these ladies. Partly, it must be admitted, because they always pay for their seats, a habit which naturally endears them to any man who writes for the theatre. Partly because they have such charming manners — to see them negotiate a tea-tray in the interval is in itself a lesson in deportment. But the principal reason for my fondness is because each one of them, though she may not know it, is a *Cephalocereus senilis*.

The resemblance is uncanny. I have one on my desk at the moment, and should not be surprised if it turned round and asked me to lend it my programme. There is the same neck, the same wind-blown, tousled coiffure — (she washed it last night, and it has not 'set' properly yet) — even the same parting.

Best of all, this is a cactus that actually has to be shampooed! It sounds like one of the things that you read in 'Believe it or not!' (I always do believe them, by the way.) But whatever your reactions to Mr. Ripley, you can take it from me that this cactus *likes* to be shampooed. Very gently, with warm soap and water. You dab it on with cotton wool, and then you blow it to make it dry more quickly. I should love to comb it too, but that would be going too far. One would feel that one was taking liberties.

§ v i

So there we are. It is to be feared that this chapter has been too rhapsodical to afford much practical guidance to the man or woman who wants to know how to grow cacti successfully. But then, in any case, those things are better learnt in textbooks. If I began to tell you about soils and composts, I should go off at a tangent, and we should never get anywhere.

The main thing to remember is that you *can* grow cacti in the city, even if you haven't much sun, or much heat, or (most important of all) much money.

The only textbook advice that I feel competent to give you concerns watering. For two reasons. Firstly because the cactus experts go on and on about it, for page after page, till you feel quite dazed and stupid. Secondly, because the cactus experts, being strictly practical people, omit to tell you that watering cacti is in itself a thrilling occupation, filled with surprises.

Let us deal with the practical side first. This watering business can be summed up in a few simple rules:

1   When in doubt, don't. For every cactus that has died of thirst, a hundred have died of drink.

2   When watering cacti in pots, don't apply the water direct to the plant, or even to the earth. Stand the pot in about two inches of water and let it soak up. Sometimes this takes as long as twelve hours. You can judge for yourself when it has reached saturation point.

3   *Re* the seasons for watering . . . from November to March, don't water them at all, in March water them once a fortnight, in April water them, and *spray* them, once a week. The idea of spraying them is to imitate the tropical rains.

During the remainder of the year, use your common sense. If it is very hot and dry they may want a little every other day. It is quite easy to tell when they do. Cacti are so human that they almost hang their tongues out at you.

There are a few exceptions to these rules, but you will learn them soon enough. The main rule is Number 1. When in doubt, don't.

That gives you all the necessary information contained in long chapters on watering by the cactus experts.

But there is one thing the cactus experts don't tell you, and that is, the *drama* of watering, particularly on the occasion of the first drink of the year. You really must know about this, for otherwise you might just put the pots in water, and then go out for a walk and miss all the thrills.

Nothing occurs for about an hour. Nothing, that is to say, except a very slight and occasional sound of gurgling, so seemingly distant that you wonder if you are imagining it.

Then, all of a sudden you sit up and take notice. Something is happening. Look at that tall spiky thing, shaped like a truncheon.[1] Before you stood it in the water it was a pale rather sickly green. But now the lower part is changing colour; the water is mounting, so swiftly that even as you watch it seems to have crept a little higher. It is like seeing the blood come back to the cheeks of someone after a long swoon. You feel that you have played the role of a saviour of life. You bend closer to observe this fascinating resurrection. You notice another miracle, and yet another.

All around you, life is flowing back to the desert.

Look at the Matinée Woman! Her hair is becoming fluffier, silkier. An hour ago she looked as if she had only just got out of bed after a long illness. Now she is getting positively perky. The lustre is returning, and the adorable curls. Soon she will be able to face the rest of the stalls with equanimity. And all her smaller sisters, all the group with little silky tufts of hair on their heads, are following her example. Before, their coiffures were

[1] *Cerous Peruvianus.*

272

like lifeless mats, now they are pom-poms, rosettes, gay and challenging.

And the Swiss Family *Lithop* ... what a transformation! When you put them in water they were as

drab and colourless as discarded bulbs or shrivelled nuts. But now they are filling out before your eyes, like poor children on a seaside holiday. Their bodies are becoming round and plump, and they are beginning to play their old game of impersonations. One of them already looks so like the pebbles surrounding him that you lift his pot out of the water in case he should be too greedy and burst himself.

Best of all is 'Shepherd's Warning', the plant that

seems to stand towards the dawn. The bloom had faded
from its cheeks, and no longer did that magic light linger
about the edges of its leaves. But the flush is returning,
slowly but very surely, and on the tip of the lowest leaf
you can see, I swear it, a faint glimmer of light. As though
in some distant desert the awakening sun had heard its
call, and had sped over hill and valley and ocean, to tell
it that it was not forgotten.

CHAPTER XVII

THE LAST CHAPTER

THE cactus epoch marked the close of what might be called the First Five Year Plan of the garden, and like the Russian dictators, I laboured under the illusion that when this Plan was completed the garden would be finished.

But no garden (nor any revolution) is ever finished. Even as I write, there are schemes afoot to enlarge the tiny pool that lies at the bottom of the rock-garden, and already, in anticipation of this event, three dripping and somewhat malodorous baskets of water-plants are causing confusion in the scullery. Nor is that all. For Mr. Peregrine is on his way, and when he arrives he will be given particulars of another Great Idea for extending the loggia and creating a vinery (don't laugh) at the end of the terrace. Already the air seems heavy with the distant thunders which will surely echo from the domain of Mrs. Heckmondwyke as soon as this Idea begins to take shape.

As if this were not enough, paving stones are being scooped up to offer a haven for thrifts and rock-daisies, another bed is miraculously being created out of nowhere, and there is even a possibility of planting a standard weeping maple in the middle of the lawn (though it would be necessary to go into retreat for several days before embarking on such a bold departure).

So it seems fairly evident that the First Five Year Plan will be succeeded by a Second, and a Third, *ad infinitum.*

However, this little book has already gone on for long enough. And now that we have reached a point where it would be possible to draw a line with some faint hope that by doing so we shall achieve some sort of 'artistic unity', what is it that prevents us from drawing that line?

Simply, I suppose, the old urge that compels us to go back to a garden, and back again, even though we know it by heart, even though the light is fading, and voices are calling us from the house, entreating us to attend to all the affairs of the world that we are neglecting.

I won't bore you by asking you to do that with me. One trip, I am sure, has been more than enough. But since we are reluctantly dragging ourselves back to the house, I feel there is just one excuse to delay our good-byes for a few moments.

We all know that a garden never stops outside the doors of a real gardener. It comes in. Not only in the shape of mud on the carpet, but of catalogues on the piano, twine round the telephone, and seed packets on the mantelpiece. In a city garden it sometimes 'comes in' even more than in the country, because space is so limited that we cannot afford to waste a single ledge that might give shelter to a window box, or to neglect the smallest cupboard in which we might force a bowl of early Roman hyacinths.

Therefore, before you walk into the hall, and out through the front door, do sit down a minute and have a glass of sherry. Thank you. That's grand. What did you say? Oh — that screen. Yes, I hoped you'd notice that, because I did it myself. What? Well, it's very nice of you to say so. No — not a bit difficult really. If you have ten minutes, I'll explain how it's done.

§ 11

I am rather glad that we have paused in front of this screen, which seems to have caught the shadow of growing flowers and trembling leaves, because on its surface is perpetuated one of my happiest memories of Allways. And between the garden of yesterday and the garden of to-day, this is one of many living links.

So let us step back into the past, to a day of spring that now seems incredibly remote, into a little garden in Huntingdonshire.

On that particular morning, the last in March, all the things which the poets have ever written about this somewhat unreliable month seemed to have come true. Tennyson's sky-blue bird had been much in evidence. So had the sky-blue scillas, which were scattered all over the garden, like pools of water painted by Monet at his gayest. And the japonica was at its best. For years I had wanted to cut one or two sprays of that japonica, but had risen above the temptation. I had looked away from it, thrust my hands deep in my pockets, and hurried out of sight, muttering things about 'spoiling the shape', and 'it will only last a week indoors'.

But on this occasion the japonica was irresistible. I had been nosing about it, off and on, all day, and when darkness began to fall, I felt that I could not do without it through the long evening. And so, in an abandoned moment, I went out, and cut a dozen sprays.

It was murder, of course. But when the japonica was set in the coarse white jug with the painted flowers, on the piano, the crime seemed worth while, for it was so beautiful. The flowers were the colour of sea-washed coral, and the leaves were as cool as jade, if you will forgive a lapse into the jargon of the 'nineties. The branches had only been thrust quickly into water, but they had arranged themselves to perfection.

As I stood there, enjoying it, I noticed that the shadows cast on the white wall were almost as lovely as the flowers. The jug was moved, very slightly. A new design of shadows presented itself on the wall. It was like playing with a living kaleidoscope. The jug was moved again. That was superb! It could not be better. For the shadow pattern had achieved a design of the most curious grace and daring. Beardsley never drew anything with a finer delicacy of line.

'What a pity such a design should be lost,' I thought. And then ... 'But why should it be lost? Why not get a pencil and trace the design on the wall? Why not? Why?'

A clatter upstairs. Drawers ransacked. Where and why do people hide things? At last! A mouldy stub of a pencil, but it will do. Clatter down again. And then, with fingers that wobble slightly, I trace the design.

It takes a couple of hours. Dinner grows cold. There is a feeling of strain throughout the cottage. But when I have finished, and move the vase away, and bring the light to the wall, there is the design, in all its living freshness, and it is hard to believe that my own fingers did it.

§III

Another glass of sherry? Good. No . . . that screen wasn't done at Allways, but it was done on the same principle. I'll explain.

Of course, one cannot go rushing round the house scribbling on all the walls behind flower vases, or relations will intervene, and conduct one with ill-concealed relief to the mad-house.

But if you play this game seriously, and take enough trouble about it, you will have vast enjoyment, and even if you *are* taken to the mad-house you can go on creating in your cell.

After the first shock of the discovery had worn off and after the village painter had come round and whitewashed

my design away, sighing heavily as he did so, I decided
that the best background for these creations would be
a screen. I had an old canvas screen, in three folds, which
had faded to a pleasant shade of dull ivory, and it seemed
probable that if shadows of flowers were projected on to
this screen, and painted in with greys and blacks and
ochres, with never a touch of colour, the result might be
very pleasing.

For various reasons, I never managed to do this at
Allways. But when I moved to London the screen came
too, and one day in March — a dull, miserable day, with
no sign of Tennyson's sky-blue bird on the horizon — I
decided to make the picture that had been so long
delayed.

The flowers would have to be cut flowers, of course.
Do you cut flowers from your London garden? I do ...
small bunches that go into miniature vases and are
usually stood in front of a mirror, to enhance their importance. In summer, the bunches increase in size, and
many is the bowl of roses that have flaunted themselves
in the hall, as though one had whole rose-gardens
tended by quantities of gnarled old men with long white
moustaches. But in March it would be asking rather too
much of so small a garden to produce a big jug of mixed
blossom. So I went out and bought them.

I went to the Caledonian market. That is one of the
consolations of being obliged to buy flowers in London,
instead of picking them. It teaches you much about the
city that you never previously suspected, and leads you

into attractive alleys and by-ways. In the old days I knew London principally by the bus routes, but now I know it by the flower shops.

So to the Caledonian Market. Most people associate this famous institution with fleas, old chandeliers, stolen silver, Bristol glass, furniture for the cook's bedroom (if you are not particularly devoted to the cook), miniatures, pinchbeck . . . and of course, the Baroness d'Erlanger. I associate it with flowers. On a lucky day, when the rain or the cold has thinned down the number of customers, you can buy, with the small change in your pocket, enough lilies to grace a fashionable wedding. You really can run amok.

I ran amok on this particular day. But the bunch for the shadow picture was a comparatively simple collection of mixed spring flowers. Daffodils, narcissi, crab-apple blossom, and some rather floppy wall-flowers. And . . . of all things . . . two branches of pine. Why pine branches? I don't know. Somehow, they seemed to complete the pattern. Even if they hadn't, it would have been hard to do without them, for there could be few more pleasant ways of spending an idle hour than to sit back with a pencil, tracing the delicate needles of a pine against a screen.

So that was that. And what had been pretty in colour became even prettier in shadow, especially after I had discovered that by using two lamps instead of one, it was possible to create a much greater variety of light and shade.

Well, I could go on about it for a long time. I could spend hours describing the mixing of the paints, the blending of the various shadow-colours, the tension which one had when tracing a particularly important stem or leaf, which was inclined to tremble in the draught. I could dilate till all's blue on the valiance with which I resisted the temptation to use colour . . . the scarlets that were eschewed, the golds that were denied, the indigoes that were rebuffed. I *am* going on about it, it seems. All the same, I hope that perhaps you may think this indoor sport worth while. It costs nothing. Only an old screen. And as long as you live, the screen will be a stage for the shadows of happy memories, the memories of the flowers you loved when you were young.

§ I V

And now you really must go? Yes, perhaps you must, if you're going to catch that train. We'll drive down together. No, it isn't any trouble. One of the reasons why it's pleasant to go into the city is because the garden seems so much lovelier afterwards.

Good-bye.

Good-bye again! Yes . . . come back when the roses are out.

Your train has gone, and I am threading my way down the crowded platform, to regain the car. Even here, among the noise and the dirt, something of the garden seems to linger with me. Even during dinner in the stuffy restaurant there is comfort in the knowledge that only two miles away from this inferno there is a patch of green, where flowers are sleeping.

Dinner is over. The clock points to ten. Too early to go home. Or is it? After all, there's watering to be done. Still, it *is* absurdly early. Perhaps a news film wouldn't be a bad idea, for half an hour.

So I pay my shilling, and sit back and watch the achievements of mankind flickering before me. Those achievements, to be frank, seem a little monotonous. Line after line of youths, in brown shirts, black shirts, red shirts, any sort of shirt . . . marching, always marching. Backwards and forwards, to the North, to the South, to the East and West. Marching with bigger and better guns, to louder and fiercer music. Marching with clenched fists or with outstretched arms, animated by the insane conviction that the fist that is clenched was made for the sole purpose of striking the arm that is outstretched. Marching, always marching, blind to the beauty that is around and above, deaf to all music save the snarl of the drum, marching to a destination that no man knows but all men dread.

No. It's a bit too much. If these are the achievements of man, give me the achievements of geraniums. Or, if you prefer it, of lupins. They at least have learnt something with the passing of the years.

So I leave the cinema, with its racing shadows of madmen and their demented leaders, and get into the car to go home. And this time the uproar and turmoil of modern civilization is bearable, because one will so soon be out of it all.

The car is caught in a traffic block. On the right is a tram, packed with tired men and white-faced women. On the left is a lorry, loaded with dripping gravel. All around are cars and buses and motor-bicycles, growling and spitting like animals on the leash, waiting to stampede as soon as the green lights give them the signal.

The lights flash, the engines roar, the wheels clank in their grooves, and we are off, twisting and turning and skidding, up the long glittering hill. Somehow I have got to the head of the procession, and lead the way up the hill, past immense cinema palaces still ablaze with neon lights, past fried-fish shops whose foetid odours drift across the roads, past dark swaying groups of men who are still leaning against the doors of the pubs, as though they hoped that some miracle might open them again. And though there is so much ugliness and squalor, it has no power over the spirit; it floats by like an evil dream from which one knows one must shortly awaken. For that is what really happens, at the top of the hill. A sudden turn to the right, down an unexpected road, and here before us are the trees, and the little house.

I switch off the engine, and listen. It is so quiet that you would think that somewhere, far away, giant doors had folded to shut out the world. It is like the contrast between two movements in an orchestral symphony. A few bars ago, the brass was blaring and the drums were

beating . . . now there is the sigh of the wood wind and the whispering of muted strings.

I step out into the little terrace, and light a match. I bend closely over the earth to see how much the seedling mignonettes have grown in the last few hours. Strangely enough, they seem to be much the same. Incredible! I strike another match . . .

But I cannot expect you to stay by my side all night, striking matches. There are limits, even to your endurance. So we will close these pages. And as we do so we both know, you and I, that if all men were gardeners, the world at last would be at peace.